YOU CAN DRA
MANGA CHIBIS

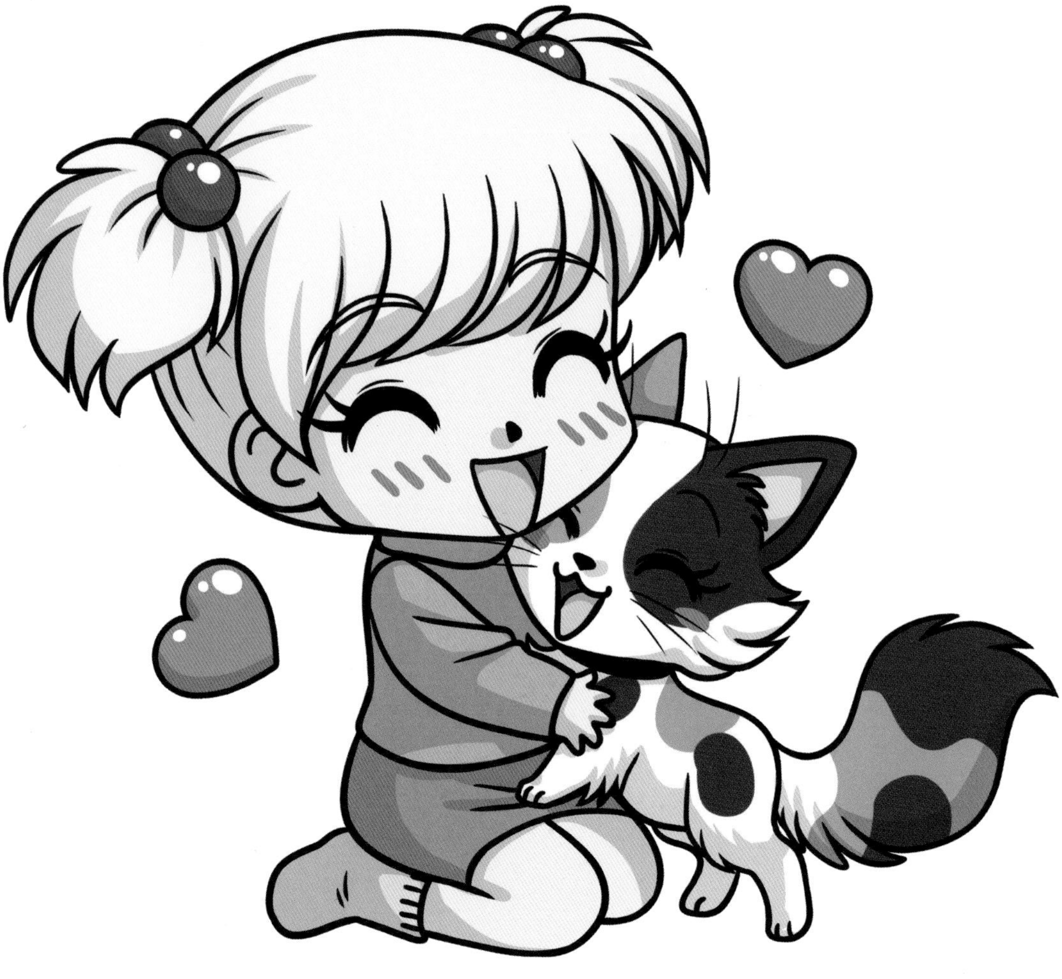

Samantha Whitten & Jeannie Lee

Walter Foster Jr.

Brimming with creative inspiration, how-to projects, and useful information to enrich your everyday life, Quarto Knows is a favorite destination for those pursuing their interests and passions. Visit our site and dig deeper with our books into your area of interest: Quarto Creates, Quarto Cooks, Quarto Homes, Quarto Lives, Quarto Drives, Quarto Explores, Quarto Gifts, or Quarto Kids.

First published in 2020 by Walter Foster Jr., an imprint of The Quarto Group.
26391 Crown Valley Parkway, Suite 220, Mission Viejo, CA 92691, USA.
T (949) 380-7510 F (949) 380-7575 **www.QuartoKnows.com**

Walter Foster Jr. titles are also available at discount for retail, wholesale, promotional, and bulk purchase. For details, contact the Special Sales Manager by email at specialsales@quarto.com or by mail at The Quarto Group, Attn: Special Sales Manager, 100 Cummings Center, Suite 265D, Beverly, MA 01915, USA.

ISBN: 978-1-63322-862-7

Digital edition published in 2020
eISBN: 978-1-63322-863-4

Printed in China
10 9 8 7 6 5 4 3 2 1

MIX
Paper from
responsible sources
FSC® C016973

YOU CAN DRAW MANGA CHIBIS

A step-by-step guide for learning to draw basic manga chibis

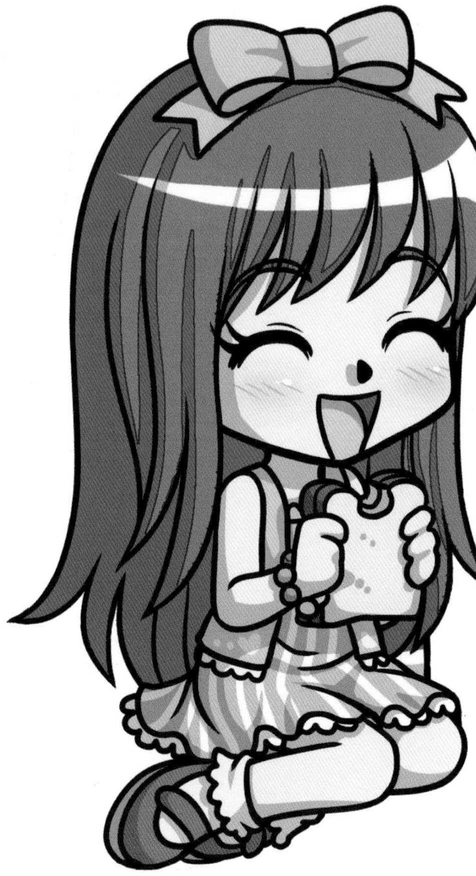

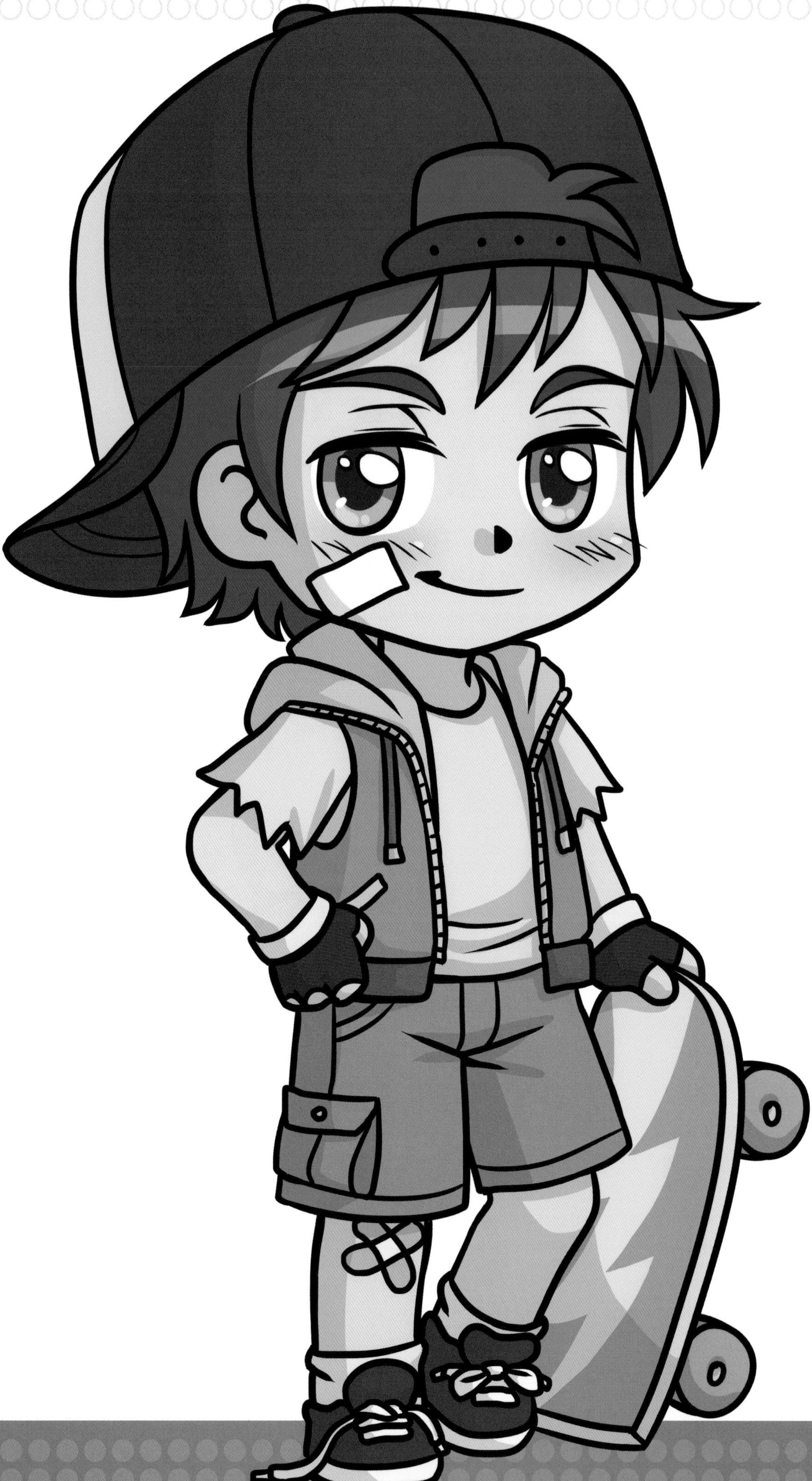

table of contents

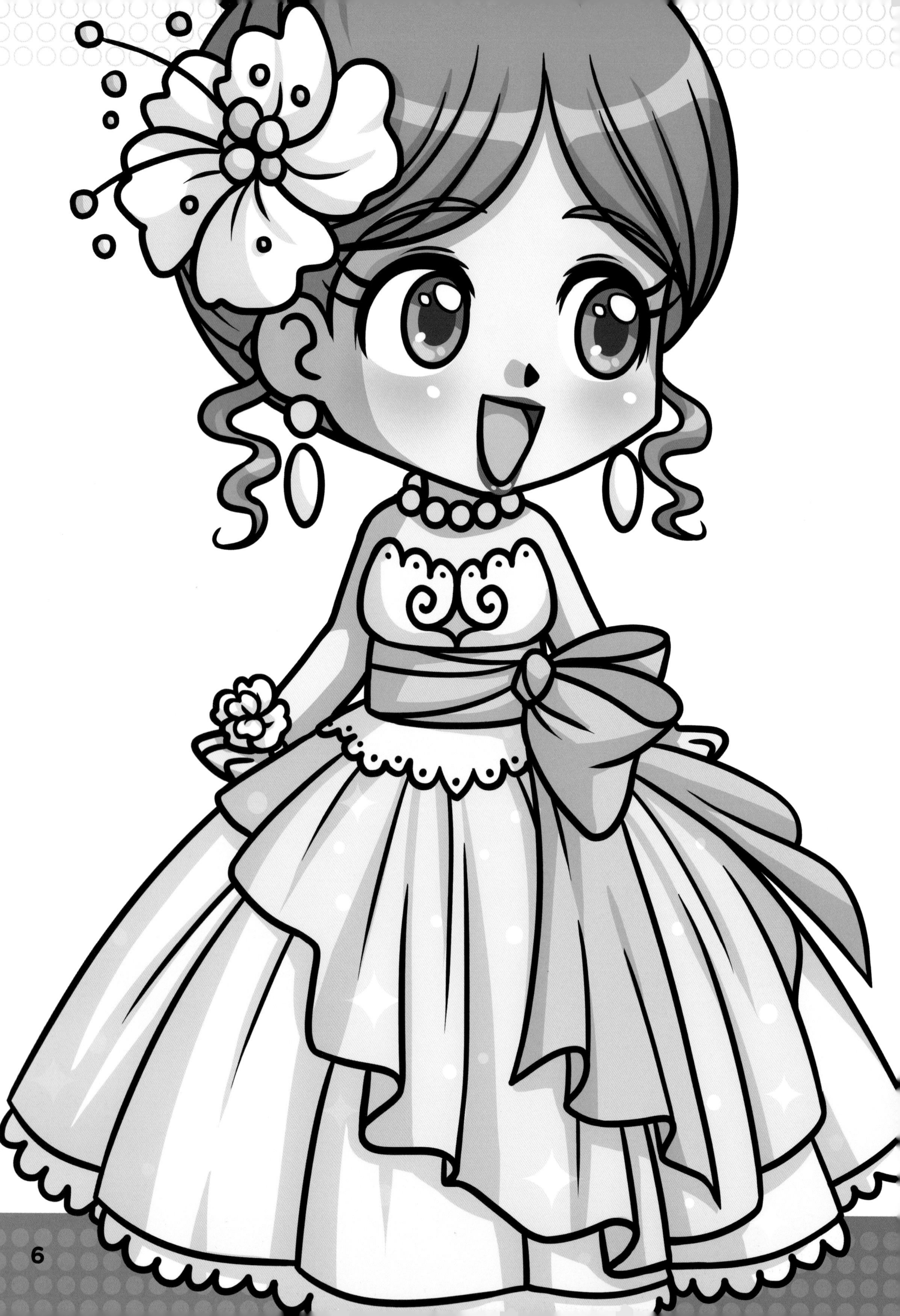

introduction

You know them well—you're reading your favorite manga or watching an anime, and suddenly a chibi appears. The word *chibi* (pronounced "chee-bee") means "little" in Japanese. Chibis are supercute caricatures of people or animals that have been shrunken and squashed into funny, childlike creatures with big heads, stubby proportions, and silly expressions. In this book, you'll learn to draw all sorts of chibis. You'll also discover exactly what gives them their "chibiness," including proportions, facial features, expressions, and poses. So what are you waiting for? A world of adorable chibis awaits! In the name of cuteness, let's dive in and get started!

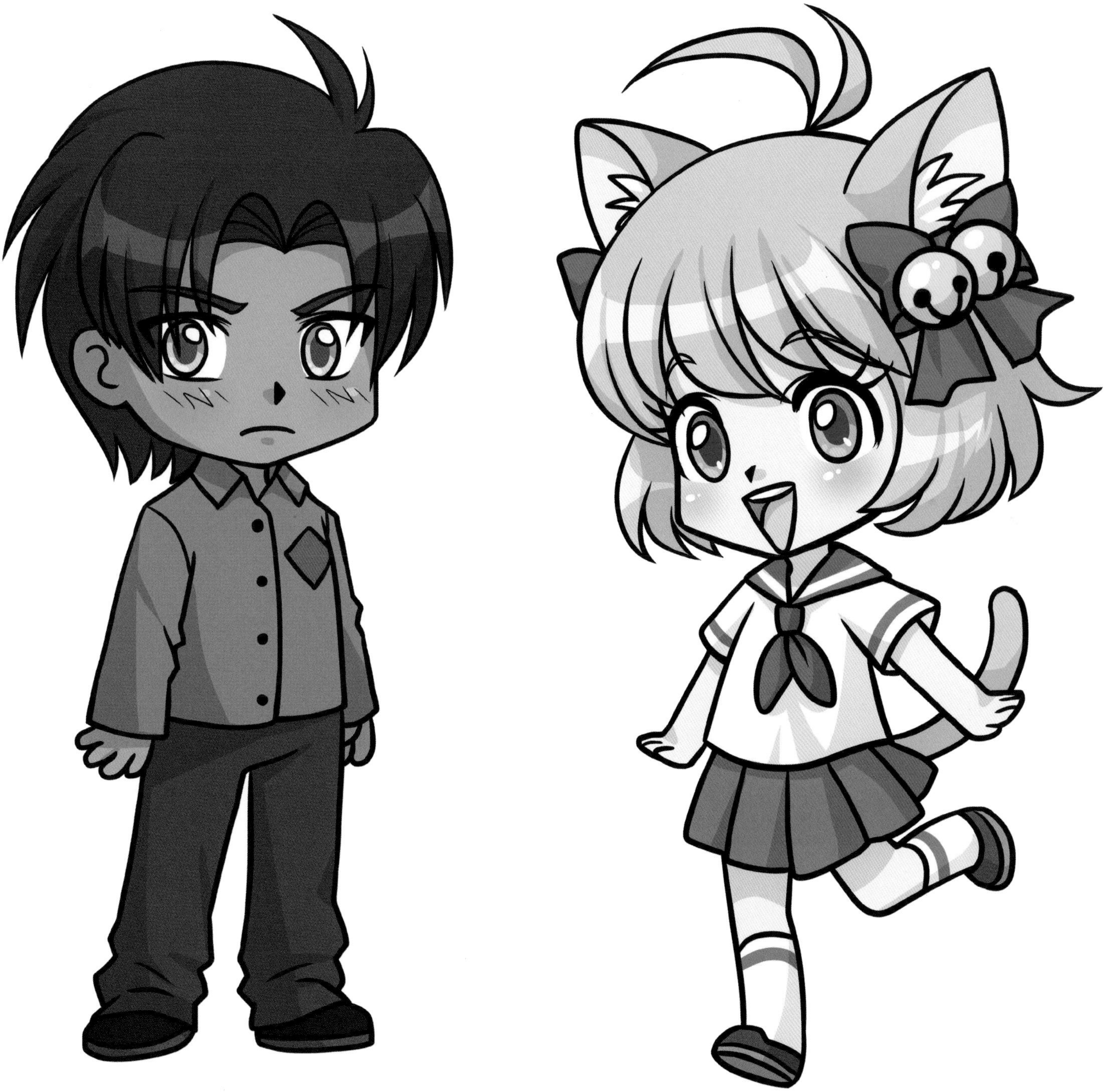

tools & materials

The artwork in this book was drawn and colored on a computer, but don't worry if you're not set up for that. You can create all of the projects featured in this book with traditional media, such as pencils, colored pencils, pens, crayons, and paints. Below are the supplies you may want to have handy to get started.

▶ **PAPER** Sketchpads and inexpensive printer paper are great for working out your ideas. Tracing paper is useful for tracing figures and creating a clean version of a sketch using a light box. Finally, cardstock is sturdier than thinner printer paper, which makes it ideal for drawing on repeatedly or for heavy-duty artwork.

▼ **BLACK FINE-LINE MARKER** Use a black fine-line marker to tighten your lines and add the finishing touch to your final color artwork.

▼ **ERASERS** A vinyl eraser and a kneaded eraser are both good to have on hand. A vinyl eraser is white and rubbery; it's softer and gentler on paper than a pink eraser. A kneaded eraser is like putty in that you can mold it into shapes to erase small areas. You can also gently "blot" a sketch with a kneaded eraser to lighten the artwork.

▲ **PENCILS** Pencil lead, or graphite, varies in darkness and hardness. Pencils with a number and an H have harder graphite, which marks paper more lightly. Pencils with a number and a B mean the graphite is softer and looks darker on paper. We recommend H or HB pencils (HB pencils are equivalent to No. 2 pencils) for sketching exercises. In general, use harder pencils (H) for lighter, thinner lines. Use softer pencils (B) for bolder, thicker lines.

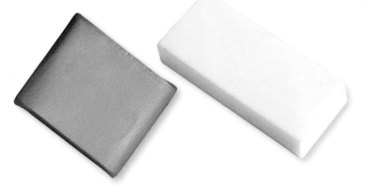

► ART MARKERS Art markers are perfect for adding bold, vibrant color to your artwork. They are great for shading and laying down large areas of color.

▲ PENS Different inks work well for coloring. When buying pens, look for "waterproof" or "archival ink" printed on the side of the pen. Look for pens that release ink consistently for inking line art over sketches.

▲ COLORED PENCILS Colored pencils layer over each other easily. They are user-friendly, and some are even erasable!

◄ PAINTS Have fun exploring acrylic, watercolor, or good old-fashioned poster paint. Make sure to research what types of paper work well with each paint.

how to use a Light box

As its name suggests, a light box is a compact box with a transparent top and light inside. The light illuminates papers placed on top, allowing dark lines to show through for easy tracing. Simply tape your rough drawing on the surface of the light box. Place a clean sheet of paper over your original sketch and turn the box on. The light illuminates the drawing underneath and will help you accurately trace the lines onto the new sheet of paper. You can also create a similar effect by placing a lamp under a glass table or taping your sketch and drawing paper to a clear glass window and using natural light.

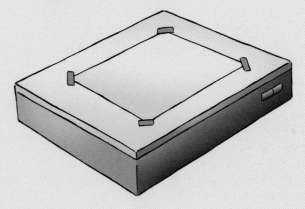

drawing techniques

WARMING UP

Warm up your hand by drawing random lines, scribbles, and squiggles. Familiarize yourself with the different lines that your pencils can create, and experiment with every stroke you can think of, using both a sharp point and a dull point.

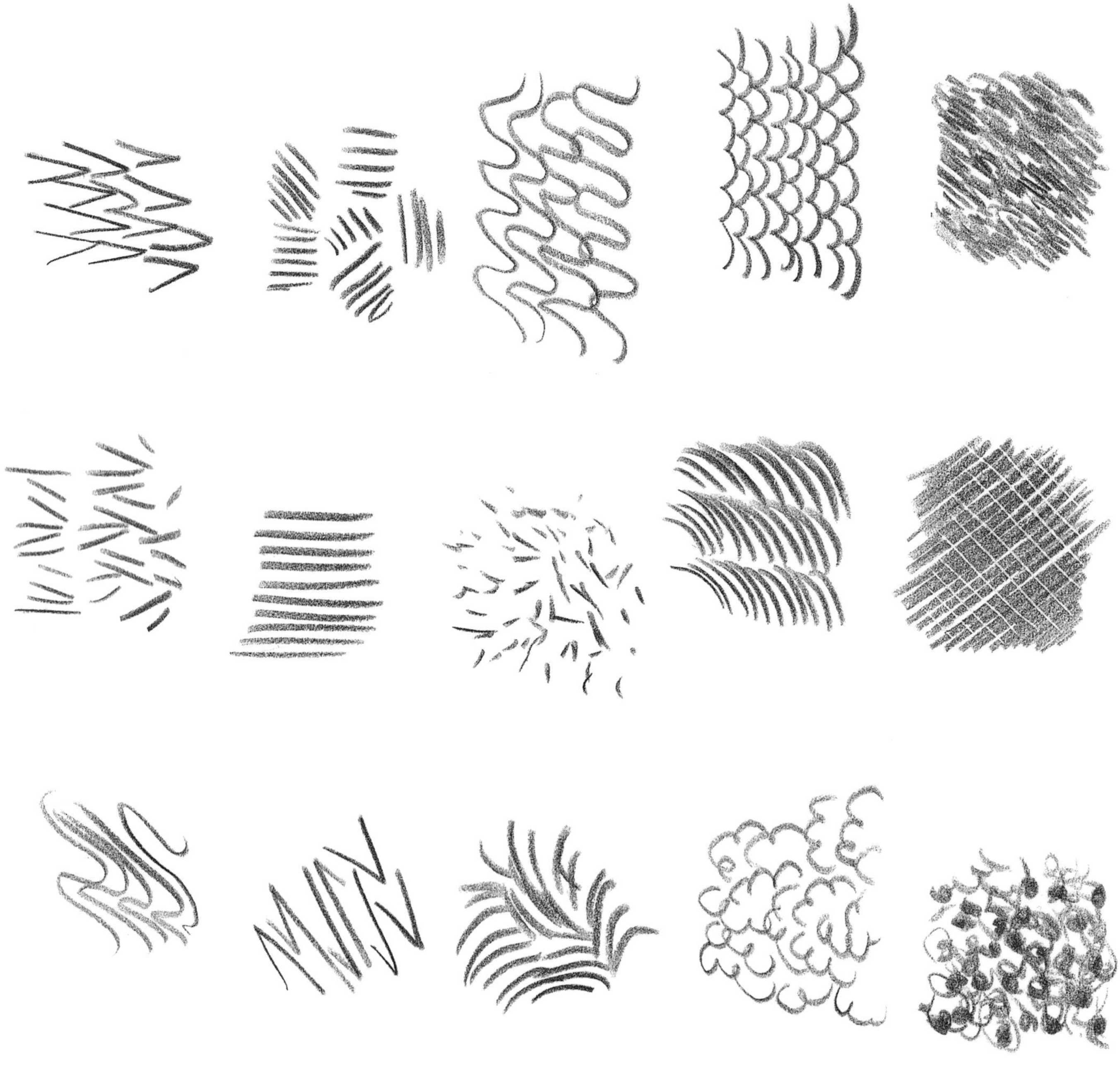

TYPES OF STROKES

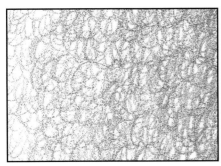

CIRCULAR Move your pencil in a circular motion, either randomly (shown here) or in patterned rows. For denser coverage, overlap the circles. Varying the pressure creates different textures.

LINEAR Move your pencil in the same direction, whether vertically, horizontally, or diagonally. Strokes can be short and choppy or long and even.

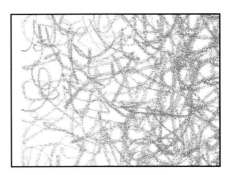

SCUMBLING Scribble your pencil in random strokes to create an organic mass. Changing the pressure and the amount of time you linger over the same area can increase or decrease the value of the color.

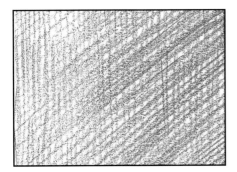

HATCHING Sketch a series of roughly parallel lines. The closer the lines are to each other, the denser and darker the color. Crosshatching involves laying one set of hatched lines over another, but in a different direction.

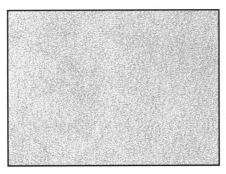

SMOOTH No matter what stroke you use, if you control the pencil, you can produce an even layer of color. You can also blend your strokes so that you can't tell how color was applied.

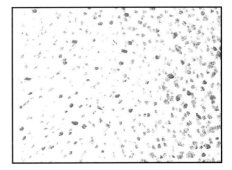

STIPPLING Sharpen your pencil and apply small dots all over the area. For denser coverage, apply the dots closer together.

COLOR basics

Color can help bring your drawings to life, but first it helps to know a bit about color theory. There are three *primary* colors: red, yellow, and blue. These colors cannot be created by mixing other colors. Mixing two primary colors produces a *secondary* color: orange, green, and purple. Mixing a primary color with a secondary color produces a *tertiary* color: red-orange, red-purple, yellow-orange, yellow-green, blue-green, and blue-purple. Reds, yellows, and oranges are "warm" colors; greens, blues, and purples are "cool" colors. See the color combinations on the next page for more mixing ideas.

THE COLOR WHEEL

A color wheel is useful for understanding relationships between colors. Knowing where each color is located on the color wheel makes it easy to understand how colors relate to and react with one another.

Yellow
Yellow-Orange
Orange
Red-Orange
Red
Red-Purple
Purple
Blue-Purple
Blue
Blue-Green
Green
Yellow-Green

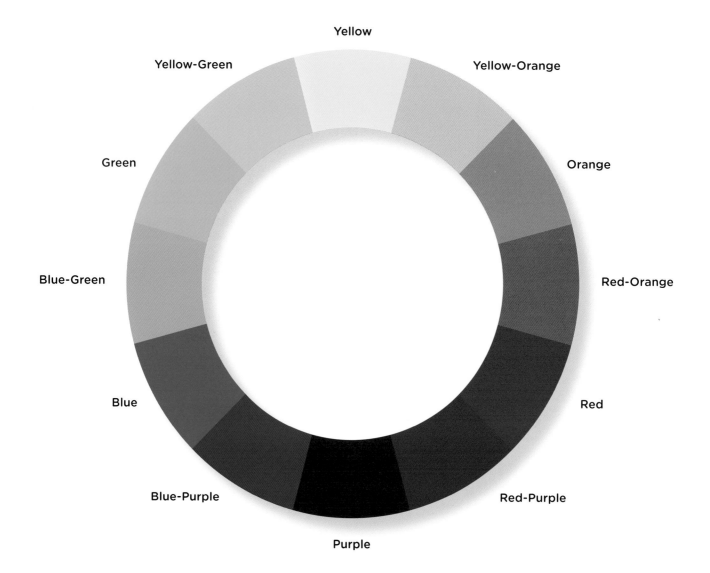

EASY COLOR COMBINATIONS

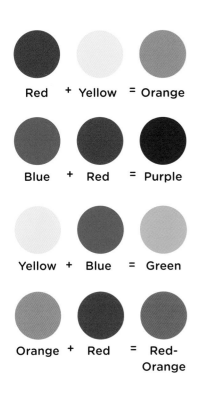

Red + Yellow = Orange

Blue + Red = Purple

Yellow + Blue = Green

Orange + Red = Red-Orange

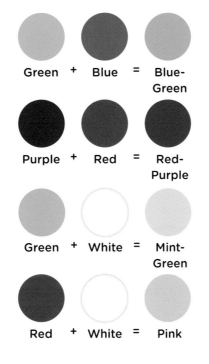

Green + Blue = Blue-Green

Purple + Red = Red-Purple

Green + White = Mint-Green

Red + White = Pink

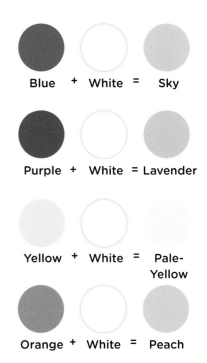

Blue + White = Sky

Purple + White = Lavender

Yellow + White = Pale-Yellow

Orange + White = Peach

ADDING COLOR TO YOUR DRAWING

Some artists draw directly on illustration board or watercolor paper and then apply color directly to the original pencil drawing; however, if you are a beginning artist, you might opt to preserve your original pencil drawing by making several photocopies and applying color to a photocopy. This way, you'll always have your original drawing in case you make a mistake or you want to experiment with different colors or mediums.

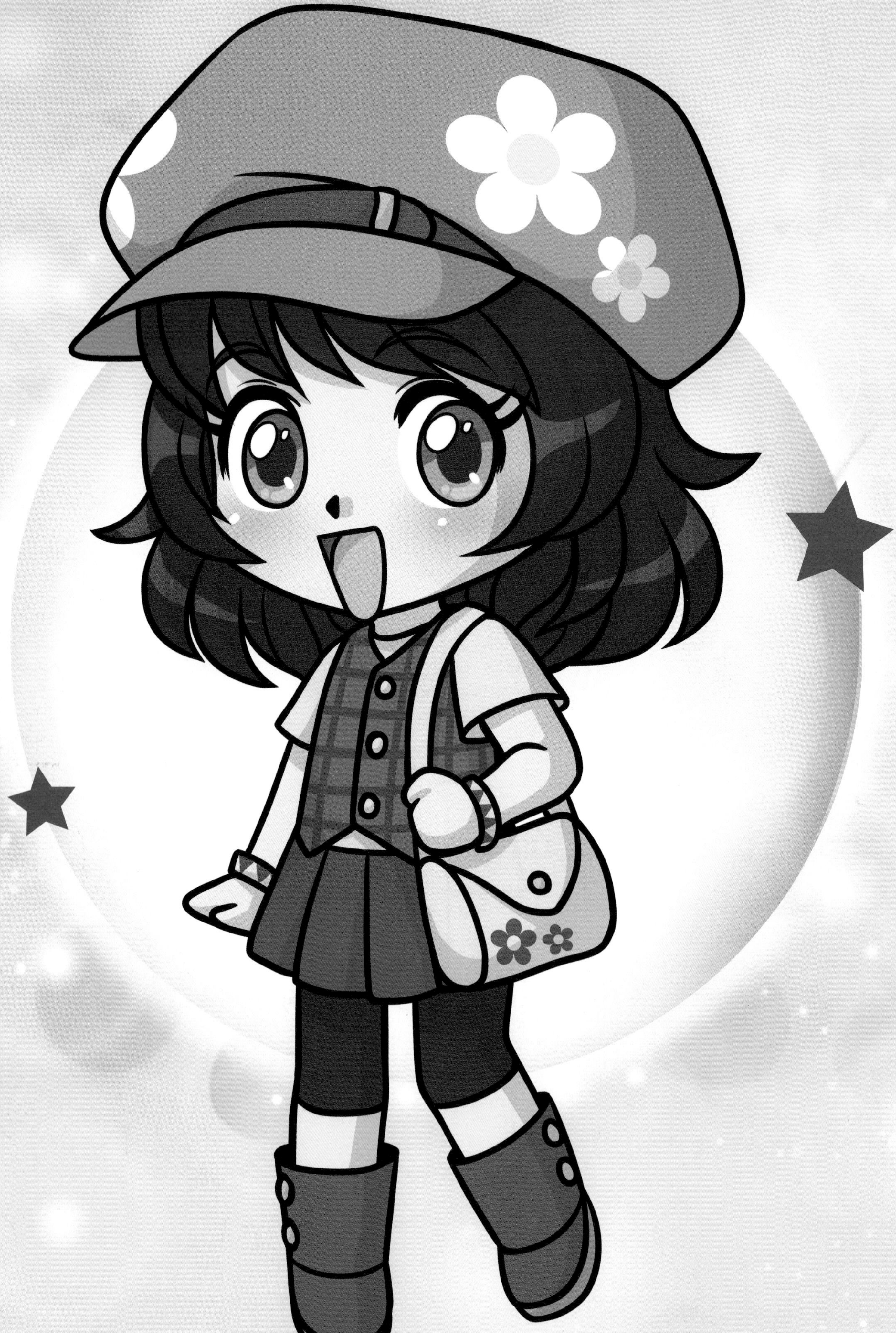

CHAPTER 1
chibi basics

what makes it a chibi?

The one attribute that sets chibis apart from other anime or manga characters is their proportions. They are squashed and simplified, and their features and sizes are altered to make them look as cute as possible. Common traits include an oversized head, a small body, stubby limbs, and big eyes.

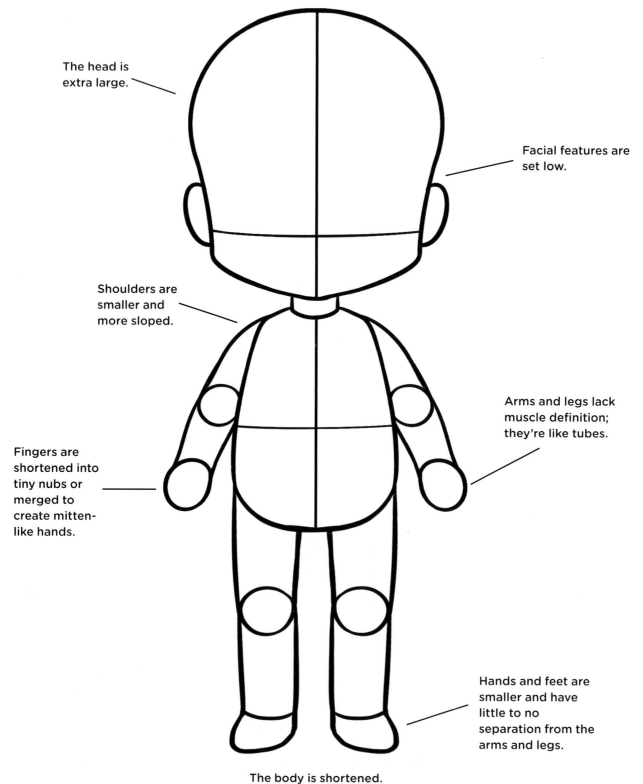

The head is extra large.

Facial features are set low.

Shoulders are smaller and more sloped.

Arms and legs lack muscle definition; they're like tubes.

Fingers are shortened into tiny nubs or merged to create mitten-like hands.

Hands and feet are smaller and have little to no separation from the arms and legs.

The body is shortened.

basic construction

These diagrams illustrate how the proportions of a normal-sized character are different from those of a chibi. A chibi's head is several times larger than a normal head, with lower guidelines for the facial features. Additionally, a chibi's arms and legs are half the typical length. Body parts are chubbier and rounder in chibi form, but this doesn't necessarily mean the character is fatter. Next to a normal figure, a chibi may resemble a child, even if it's not. A chibi character is merely a simplified version of a normal-sized character.

PRACTICE MAKES PERFECT!

Use the templates beginning on page 72 to practice drawing a wide range of chibi characters. You can either scan the templates to your computer and print them out or photocopy them from the book.

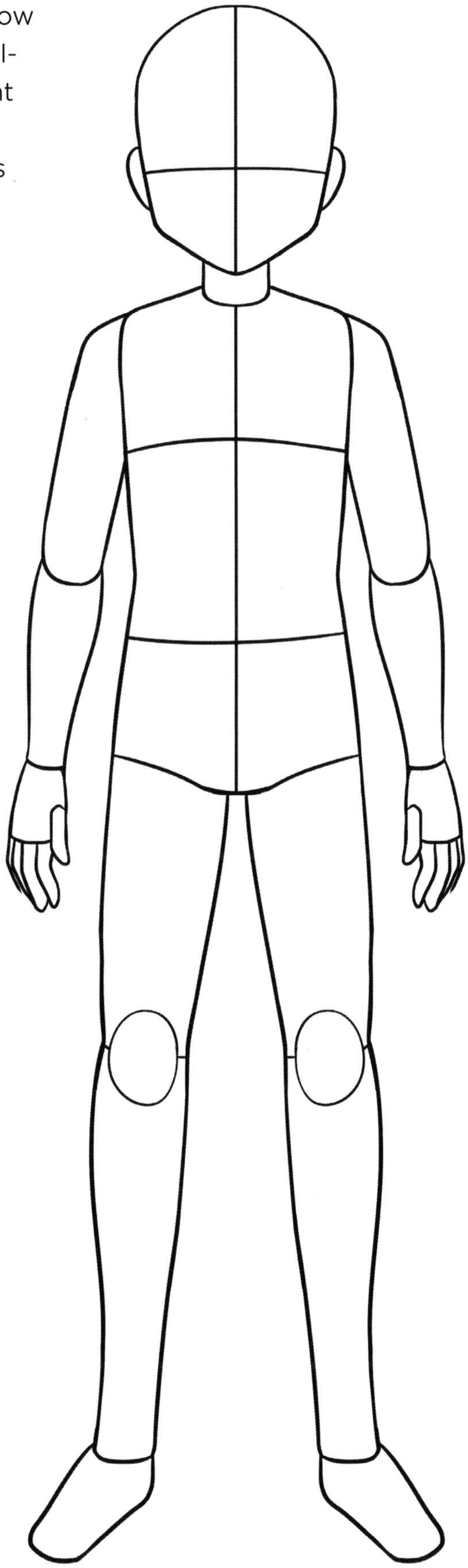

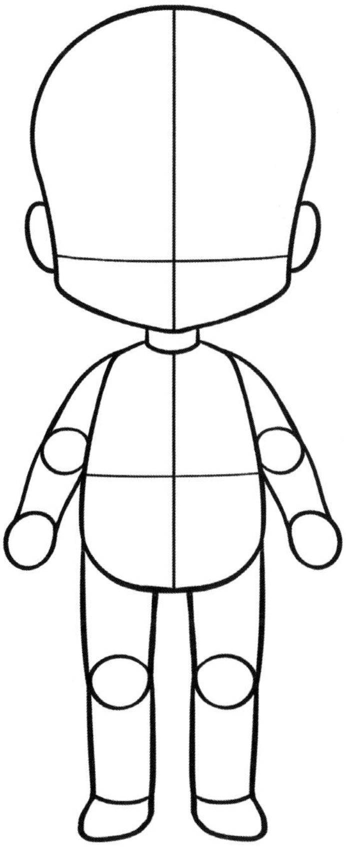

chibi giRL tRaits

Girl chibis are commonly drawn hopping, skipping, or floating in midair to demonstrate that they're light on their feet. The "pigeon-toe" pose is common for female chibi characters. Toes pointing inward give the character a coy demeanor. In contrast to a male chibi body, females may also have hourglass figures.

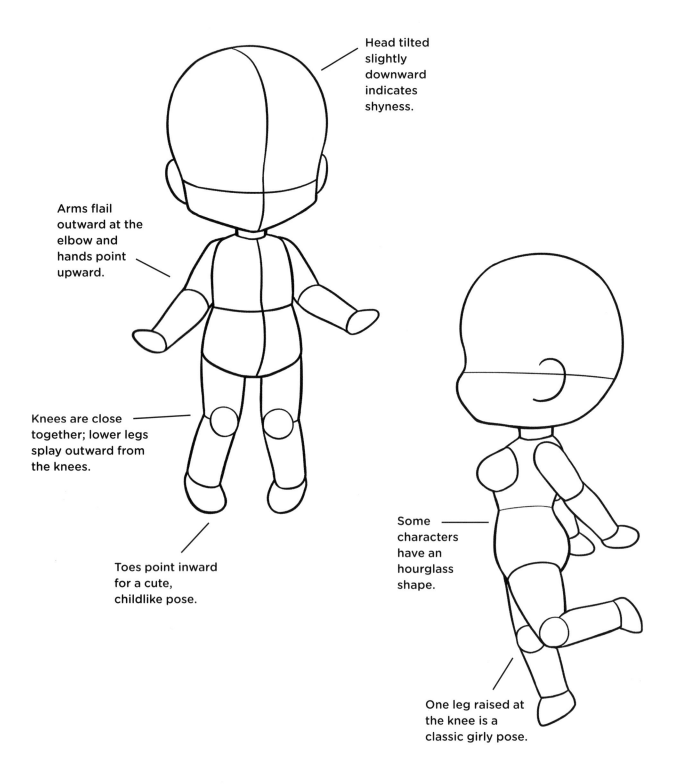

Head tilted slightly downward indicates shyness.

Arms flail outward at the elbow and hands point upward.

Knees are close together; lower legs splay outward from the knees.

Toes point inward for a cute, childlike pose.

Some characters have an hourglass shape.

One leg raised at the knee is a classic girly pose.

breaking it down: sakura

To see the differences between a normal figure and chibi figure more clearly, let's take a look at them side by side. The differences between the two figures are many, but they still look like the same character because they share traits unique to Sakura, including hairstyle, colors, outfit, and body language. It's important to figure out which traits to keep the same and which to exaggerate so your character looks like the same person whether it's in normal or chibi form.

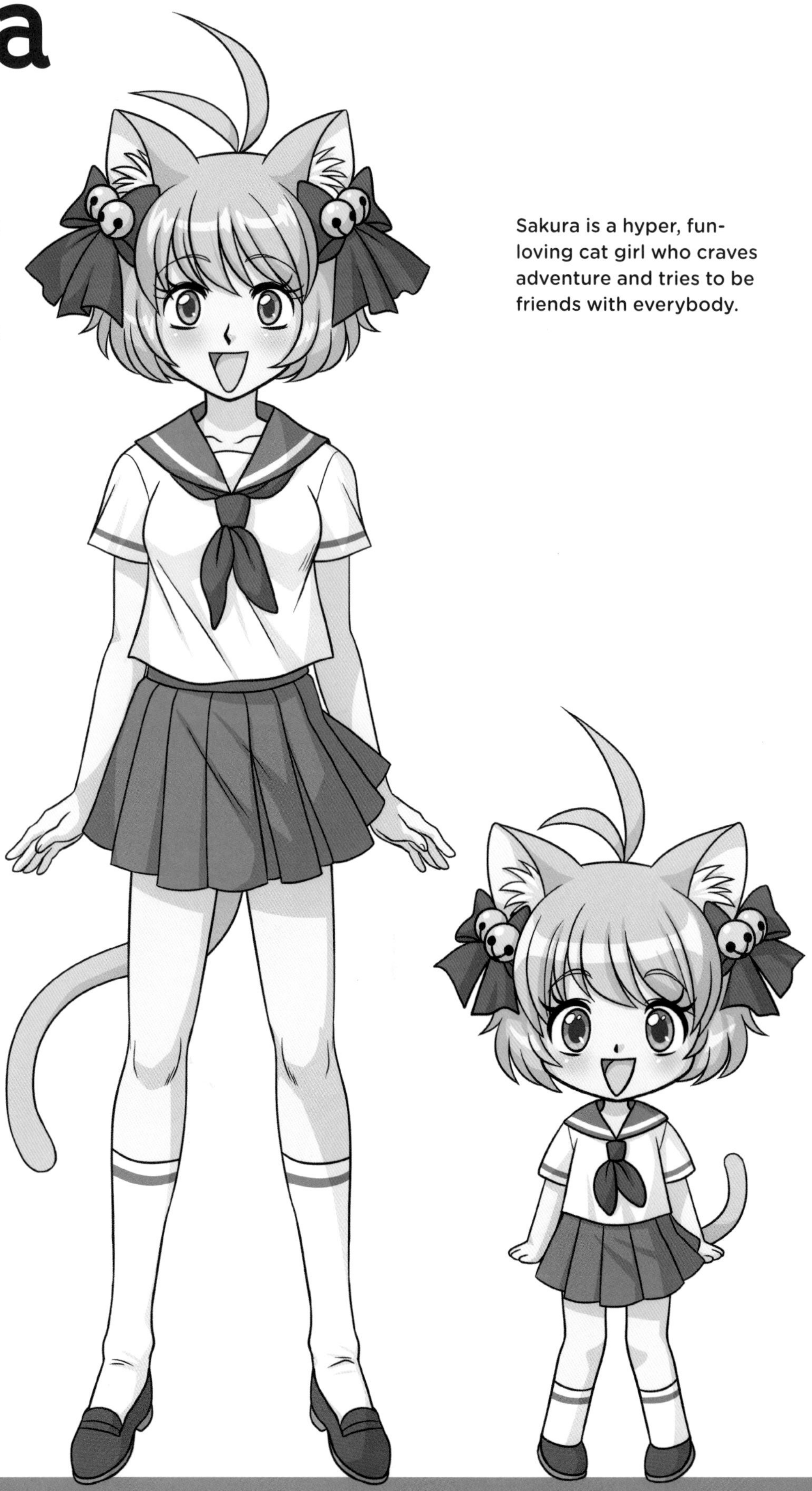

Sakura is a hyper, fun-loving cat girl who craves adventure and tries to be friends with everybody.

HEAD

The chibi head is much wider than the head on the normal figure; moreover, the facial features are placed much lower on the head. A chibi barely has a chin, and the eyes are larger and set wider apart. The eyes are also positioned lower on the head, which means the nose, which is smaller, is between the eyes instead of below them. Some artists omit the nose altogether.

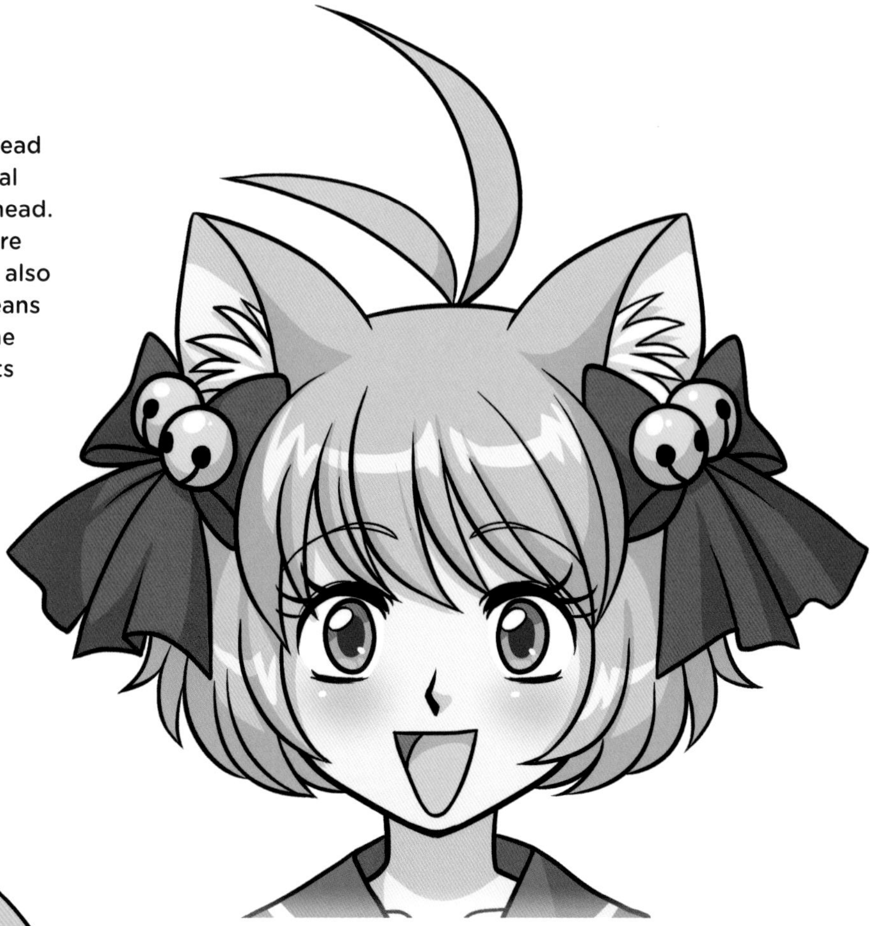

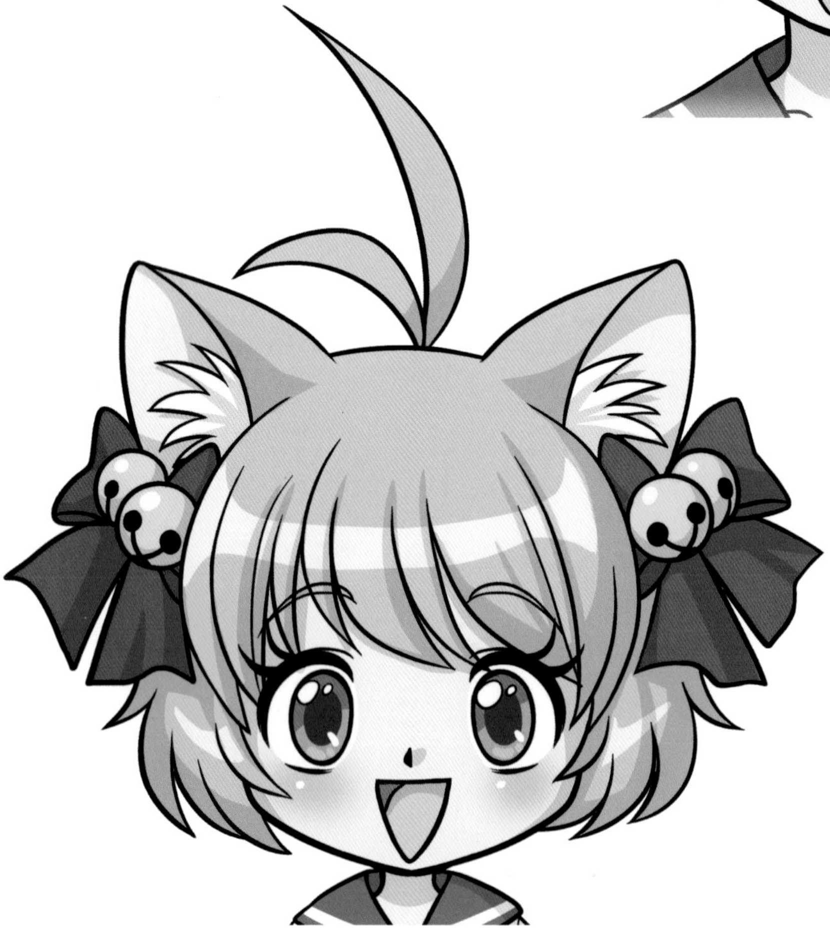

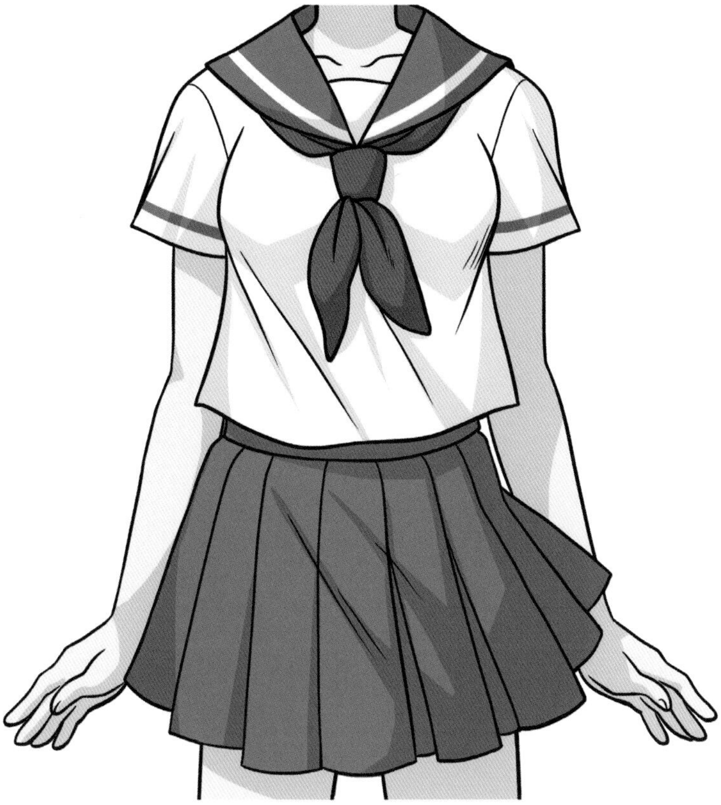

BODY

The chibi body transforms from a rectangle to a pear shape (wider on the bottom and narrow at the shoulders). The arms show no definition at the elbows, and the hands are wedges with lines to indicate stubby fingers. The chibi chest is much smaller, and there are fewer folds in the clothing. Notice how the pleated skirt becomes little more than wedges of color. The tail is shorter and only has a single curl.

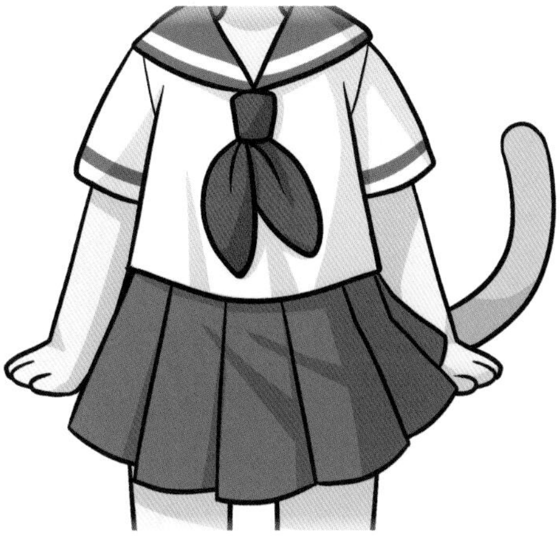

LEGS

Goodbye legs, hello noodles! Avoid adding too much detail to chibi legs. In chibi form, the thigh muscles and lower legs disappear completely—only shading indicates the knees. Think of chibi legs as long tubes with bends in the middle. The shoes are smaller and stubbier, as well. Chibi Sakura adopts a pigeon-toe stance, with her knees close together and legs angled outward.

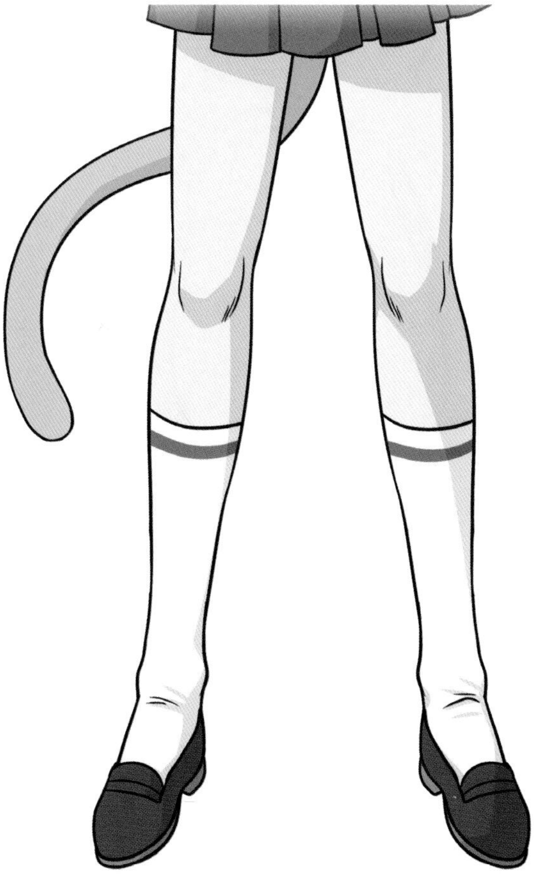

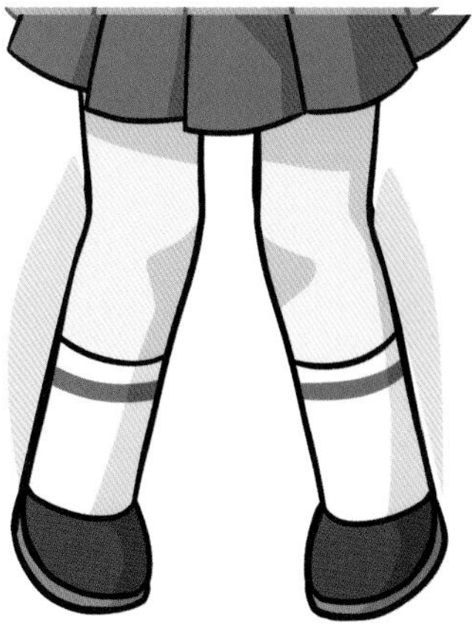

chibi boy traits

Chibi boys are often shown in strong, firm poses. For example, he can stand with his chest puffed out, legs slightly apart, and feet planted firmly on the ground. Arms are often drawn in strong or casual poses, with the hands on the hips or the arms hanging straight down. Hands can be drawn as fists, which are merely ball shapes. The body shape is rectangular, or for a more muscular character, you can make the chest wider and the hips narrower. Muscles are often smoothed down, as definition is contrary to the chibi style—unless your character happens to be a super body builder!

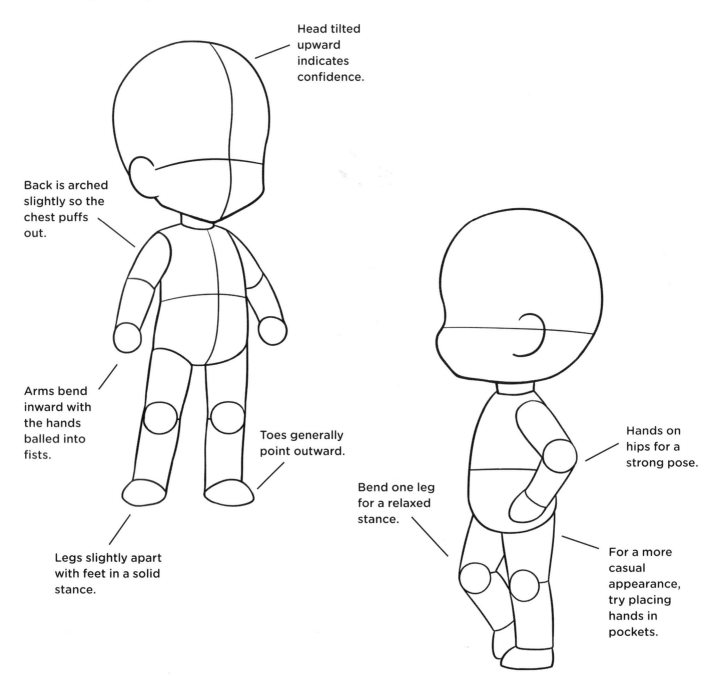

Head tilted upward indicates confidence.

Back is arched slightly so the chest puffs out.

Arms bend inward with the hands balled into fists.

Toes generally point outward.

Legs slightly apart with feet in a solid stance.

Bend one leg for a relaxed stance.

Hands on hips for a strong pose.

For a more casual appearance, try placing hands in pockets.

breaking it down: takashi

Now that we've changed Sakura into a chibi, let's move on to her grumpy friend, Takashi. The breakdown is pretty much the same, although there are slight differences.

Nobody works harder than Takashi. He takes his schoolwork very seriously and can be a bit grumpy sometimes.

HEAD

Takashi's chibi head is wider and larger overall. The eyes are oversized, set wider apart, and placed lower on the head, while his ears are rounder with simplified details. The nose is a small dot. Flushed cheeks is a universal chibi trait.

BODY

Takashi's body is wider at the bottom and narrow at the top, with slim, sloping shoulders. In chibi form, he appears to be a little chubby in the belly, which gives the look of having "baby fat"—another childlike feature common in chibi styles. The folds of his clothing have also been refined, and his hands are also balled into little fists.

LEGS

The knees have vanished again! Takashi's chibi legs are straight and simplified. Similarly, clothing folds are smooth. Takashi's chibi feet are the same shape as Sakura's, but the pose is different.

basic chibi face
FRONT VIEW

Compared to a normal face, chibi facial features are larger and sit toward the bottom half of the face. The forehead is large, and the eyes are wider and set below the center of the face. Chibi eyebrows arch more dramatically around the shape of the eyes, resulting in a wide-eyed, childlike expression. The chibi nose is a tiny triangle, and the mouth is shorter. Also note the rounder, wider head; flattened chin; and short, thin neck. Use the blue guidelines to measure the differences in proportion and placement between the upper and lower halves of each face.

SIDE VIEW

In the side view, also called the profile view, the facial features are still compact and placed lower on the face, resulting in a larger, broader forehead. The jawline and chin are smoothed out and simplified, which makes the chibi character appear shorter and pudgier. The head is more circular, whereas the eye and eyebrow are larger and more pronounced. A small protruding bump indicates the nose, and the mouth and neck are both shorter. You'll also notice the ear doesn't connect to the edge of the jawline.

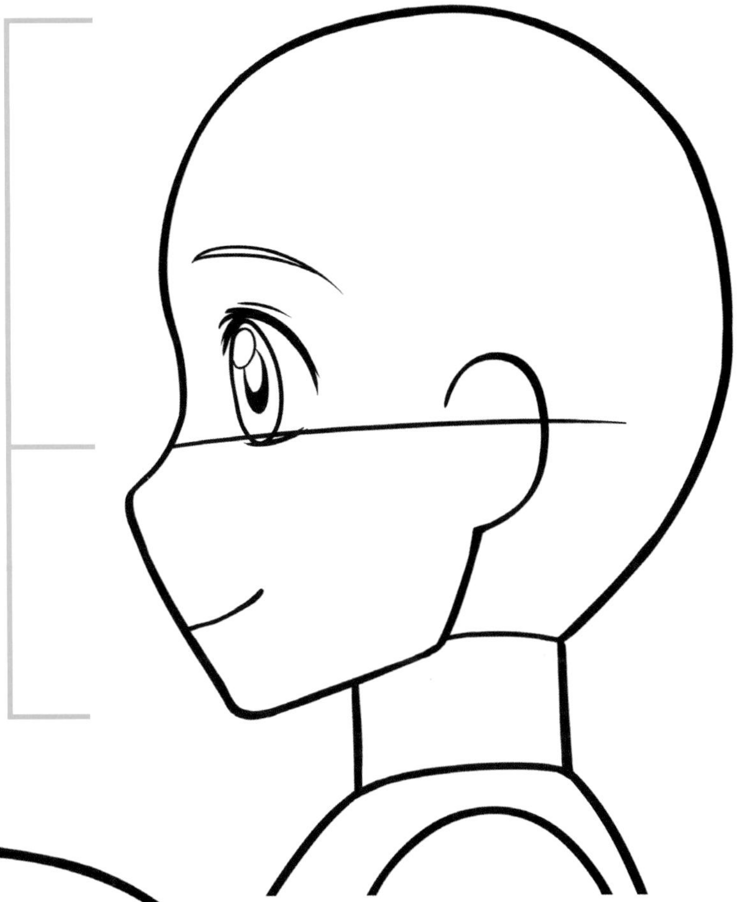

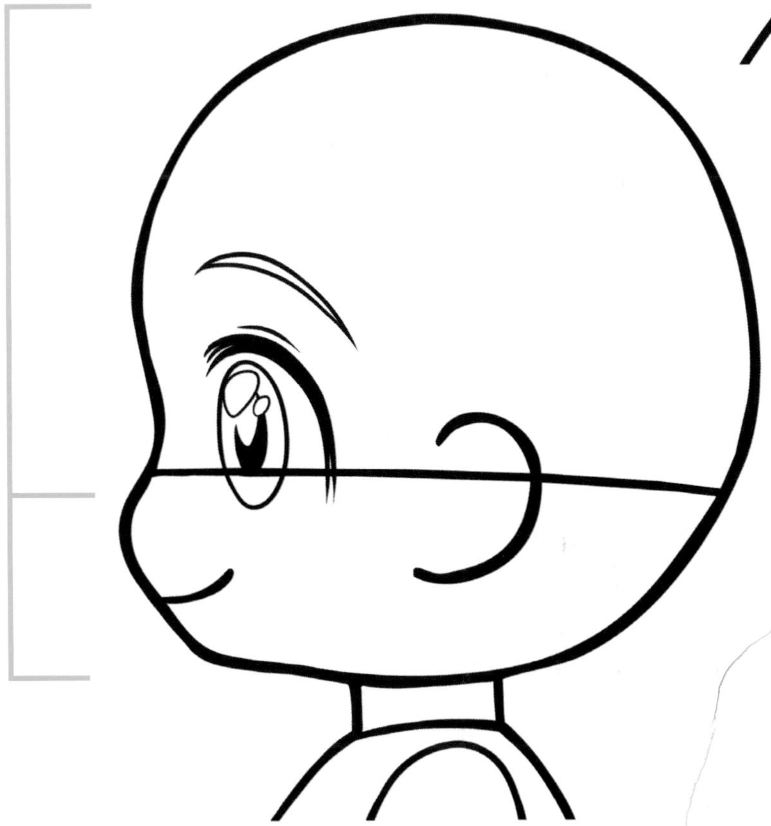

average chibi body

Chibis come in all shapes, sizes, and proportions, but the most common body shape is shown below. In this example, the body and legs are approximately the same height, and the head is larger than both! Artists often invent their own measurements and proportions, and you should do the same. If your chibis do start to resemble normal-sized children, tweak the image. Making the head larger is a good first step.

The four most common angles are the front, side (profile), back, and three-quarter views. Note how the shape of the head changes from each angle, and how the arms and legs indicate which direction the character is facing. Even if the angles change, the character still appears to be the same shape, height, and size from all views.

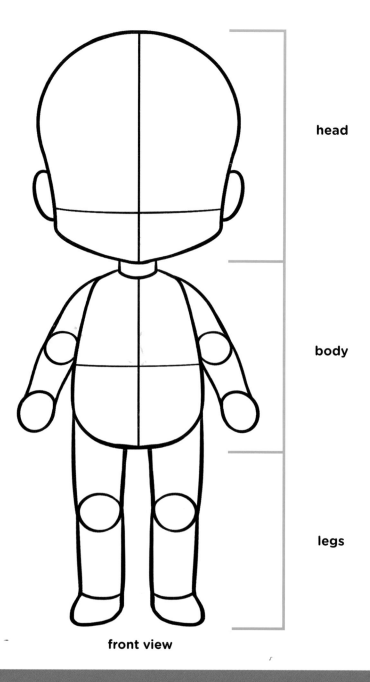

head

body

legs

front view

side view

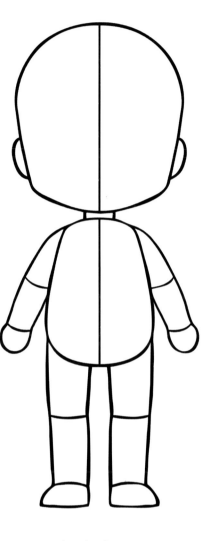

back view

3/4 view

tip

Use basic shapes, including circles, cylinders, and guidelines, to start your drawings. Skipping this step may result in your characters appearing out of proportion.

chibi giRL face

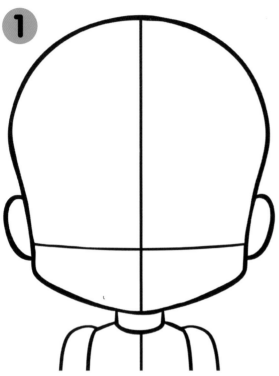

1

Sketch the basic head shape and guidelines. The ears are shown here even though the hair will cover them. It's always good to draw the shapes for all of the features, even if they aren't visible in later steps.

2

Draw the eyes, eyebrows, and eyelashes. Next draw the hair, mouth, nose, and accessories. Pay attention to how the guidelines help establish where the other details sit.

3

Erase unnecessary sketch lines and add your base colors, followed by shading and highlights. Add dark blue pupils to the center of the eyes along with highlights so they seem full of energy. For added flavor, give your chibi girl a few freckles. The options for adding characteristic flair are many. Use your imagination!

chibi boy face

1

Sketch the basic head shape and guidelines.

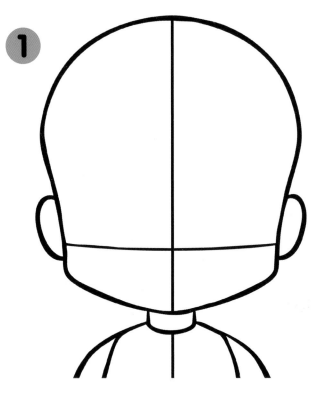

Add the eyes, noticing how the boy's eyes rest directly on the centerline. He doesn't have eyelashes, but he does have thick eyebrows. Next, add the nose, mouth, and hair, with two little tufts standing on end.

2

3

Erase unnecessary guidelines. Then add your colors and highlights. You can give the boy brown hair and green eyes, or any colors you like. Add highlights to his hair to make it appear shiny and round. With dark green pupils and brighter highlights, his eyes seem alert. Add a pink flush to his cheeks.

chibi girl face: side view

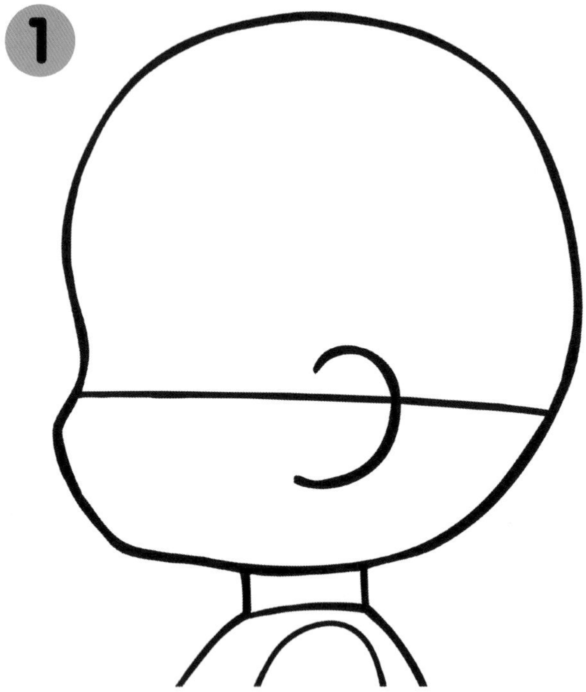

Begin with basic shapes and guidelines, including a rounded head and slight bump for the nose. The chin is short and slightly angles outward. Because this is a profile view, the ear sits near the center of the head.

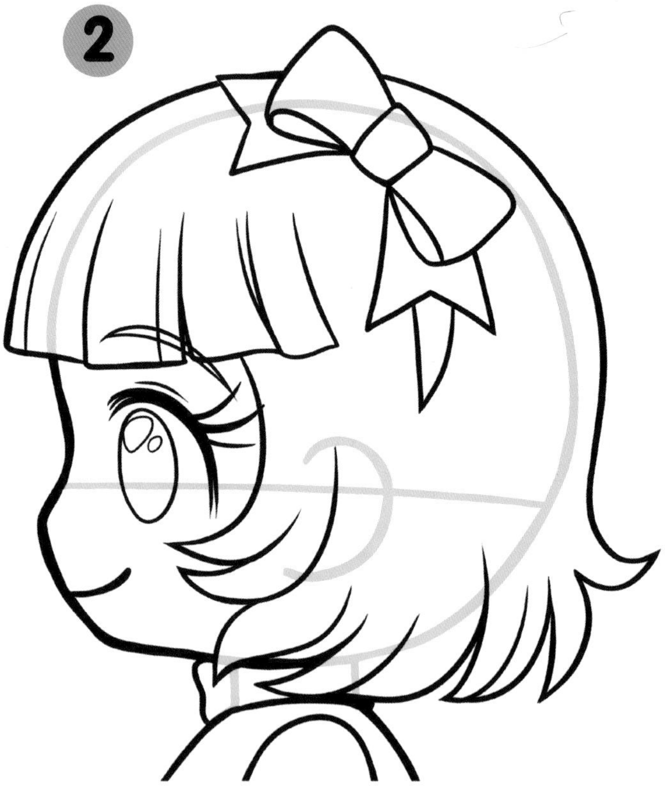

Draw the eye first, placing it toward the lower half of the face. Next, add in the details, including the mouth, hair, and accessories. Don't get discouraged if it takes some practice to capture the style.

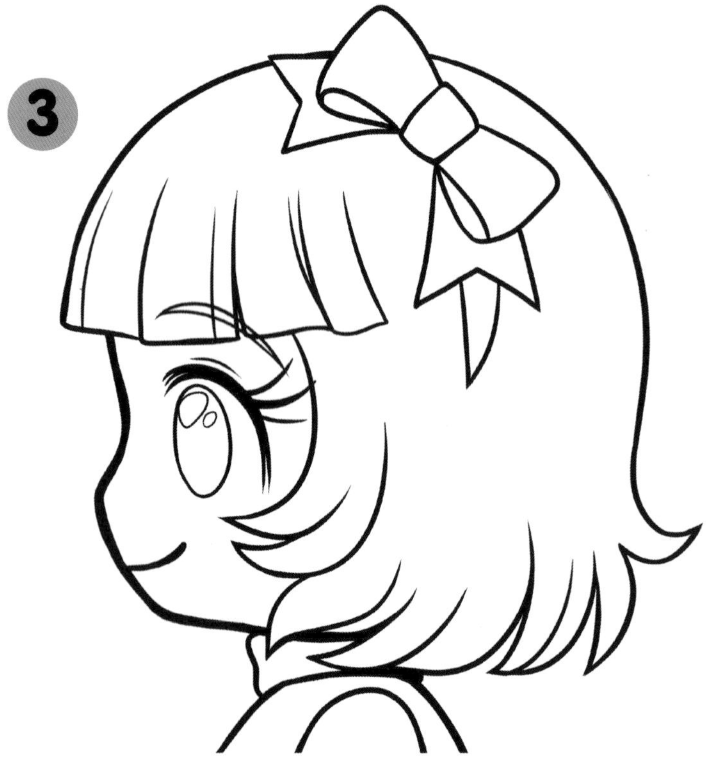

Erase the guidelines and clean up your line art.

Match the colors and highlights to
the front view chibi on page 31, or
add all new colors if you like.

chibi boy face: side view

1

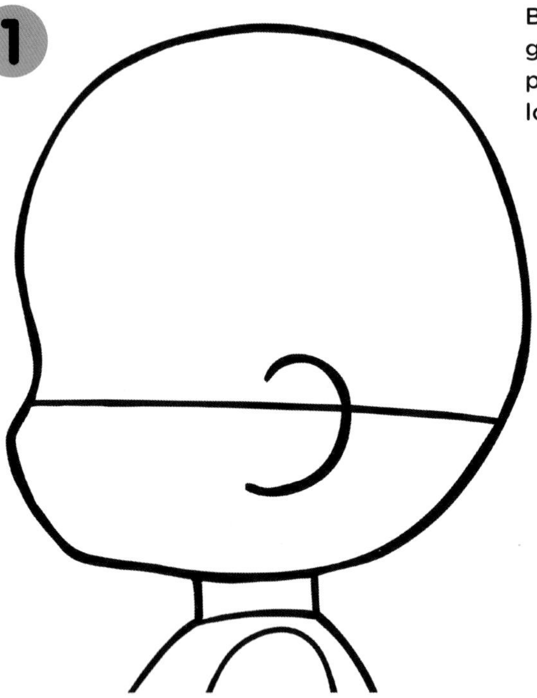

Begin as before with basic shapes and guidelines. As with the front view on page 33, add slightly more space on the lower half of the boy's face.

2

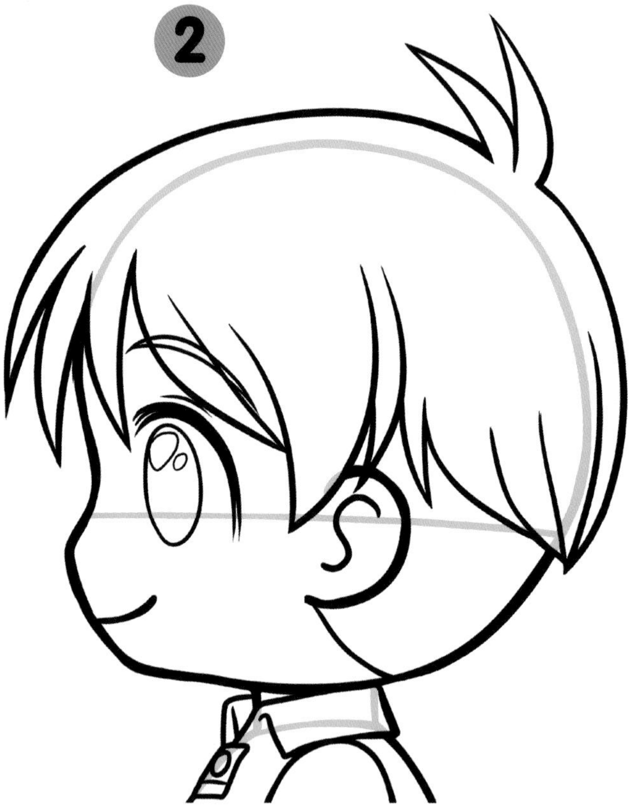

Reference the front view of the boy's facial features, hair, and clothes as you draw him at a different angle. Pay attention to where the top of the hair is in relation to the guideline.

3

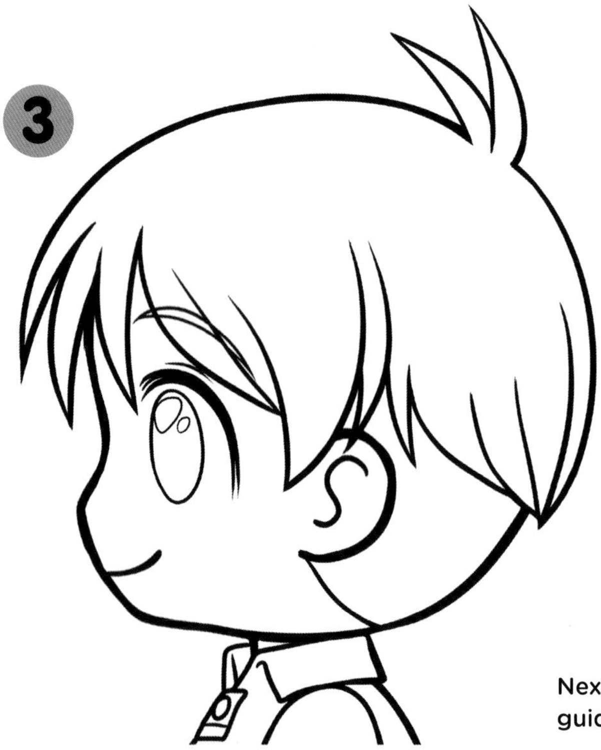

Next, erase the basic shapes and guidelines, and clean up your line art.

4

Reference the front view drawing as you color,
shade, and highlight. Add a smooth highlight arc
on the head to create depth. Don't forget to add a
slight flush to his cheek as a finishing touch.

chibi body: front view

The front view is ideal when first designing a character. To draw a more lively front view, try moving body parts or changing stances. Raise the character's arms, bend its legs, or give it a quirky expression. There are many ways to add feeling to a seemingly straightforward pose. In this example, our chibi girl has been caught by surprise!

First, draw the basic shapes: cylinders, circles, and guidelines.

Draw the facial features, hair, clothes, and accessories.

1

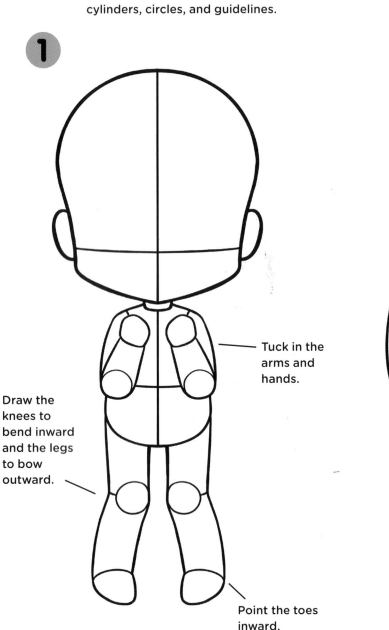

Draw the knees to bend inward and the legs to bow outward.

Tuck in the arms and hands.

Point the toes inward.

2

3

Add solid colors before shading or highlighting. Color in the pupils and add highlights to give the eyes depth. Add a blush to her cheeks, if you like.

chibi body: side view

Use guidelines to keep the side view chibi from appearing flat. There are tricks to add dimension. For example, draw the arm and leg on the opposite side so they are visible. Always think three-dimensionally!

1

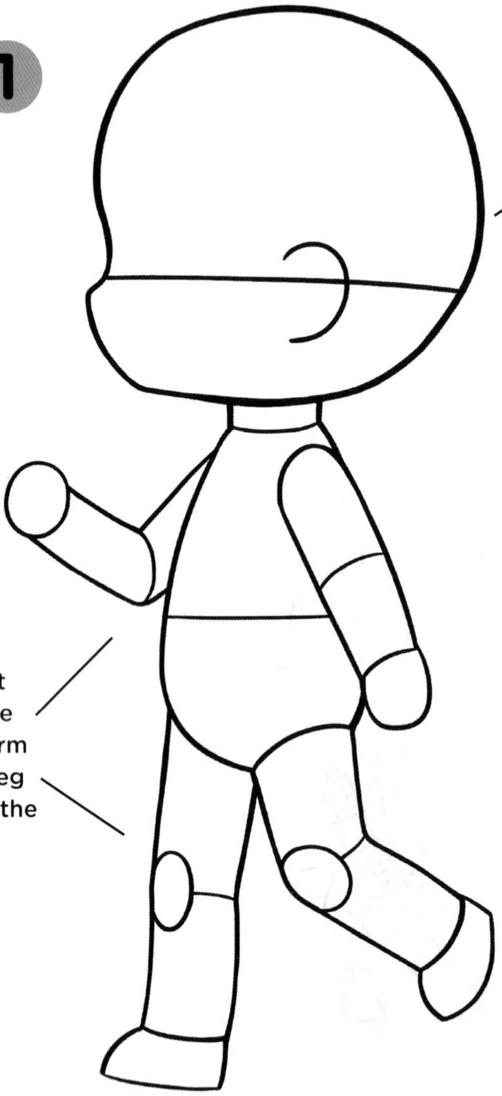

Draw the basic shapes and guidelines. Remember: Heads are round!

Notice that you can see the right arm and right leg even from the left side.

2

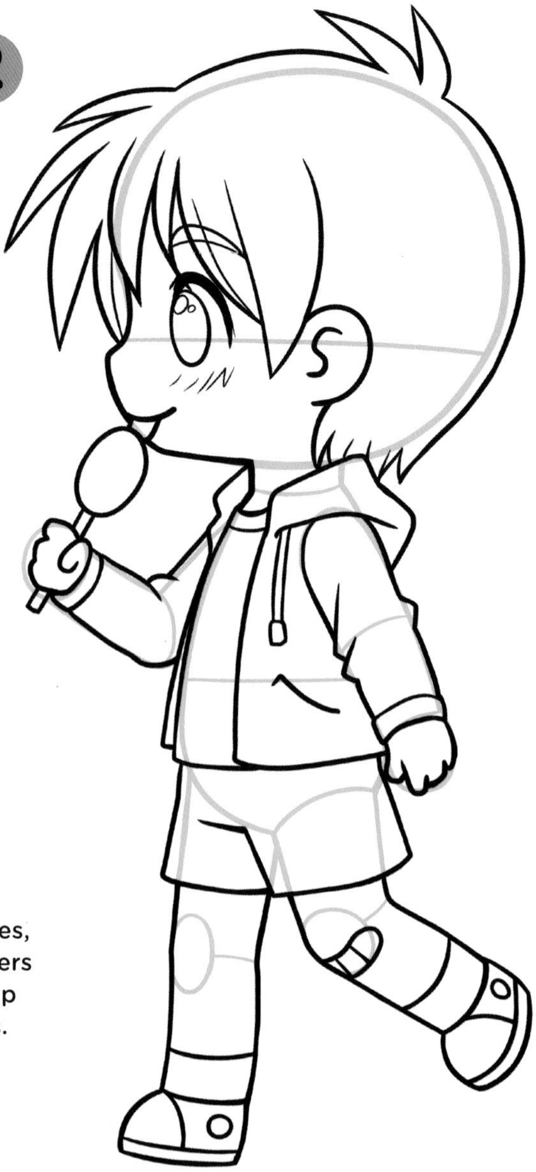

Draw the facial features, hair, clothes, and fingers so they appear to wrap around the guidelines.

3

Add color, shading, and highlights.

EXERCISE YOUR CREATIVITY!

Remember that fantasy characters can have features that are unnatural in the real world. Why *not* make their hair blue and their eyes yellow? These unexpected surprises make your character unique and fun.

chibi body: back view

The back view is essentially the same as the front view. The basic shapes are the same—only the details are different.

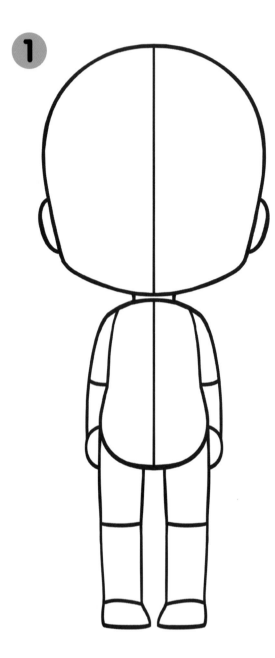

1

Draw the basic shapes, noting the absence of facial feature guidelines.

2

Add the hair, ribbons, and dress.

3

The back view starts to make sense after adding color. Don't forget to add shading to the hair, skin, and dress. Add highlights to the hair to give it depth.

tip

Although this chibi girl is standing still, you can give her pose movement with a few tricks. Notice the way the ribbons in her hair and on her dress sway a bit to the right. Her dress blows to the right, as well, which gives the illusion that she's standing outside on a breezy day.

chibi body: 3/4 view

Now that you've mastered the front, side, and back views, let's sketch Sakura at a three-quarter view.

1

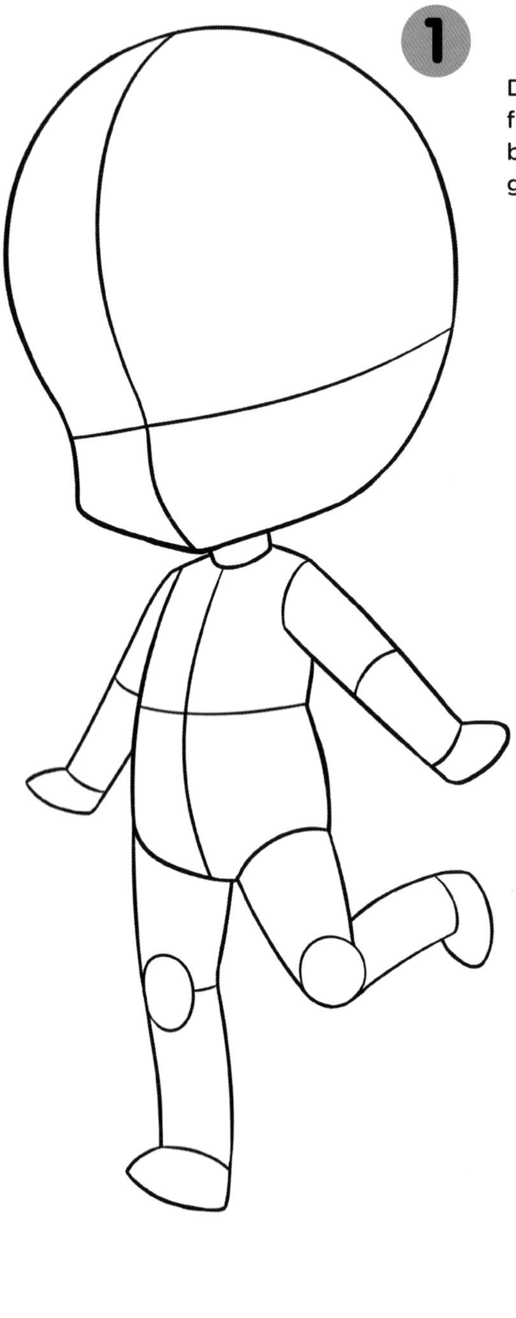

Draw Sakura in a frolicking pose with basic shapes and guidelines.

2

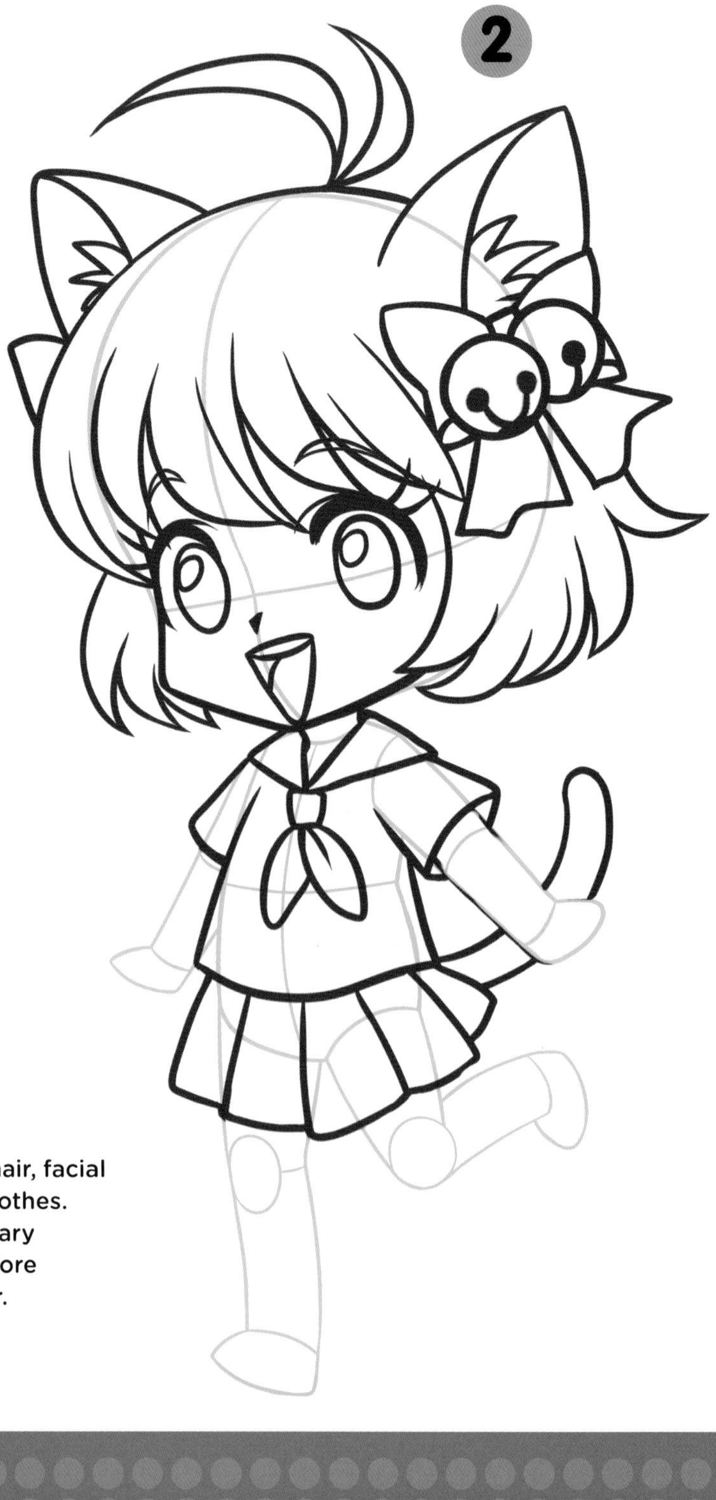

Now draw the hair, facial features, and clothes. Erase unnecessary sketch lines before moving to color.

3

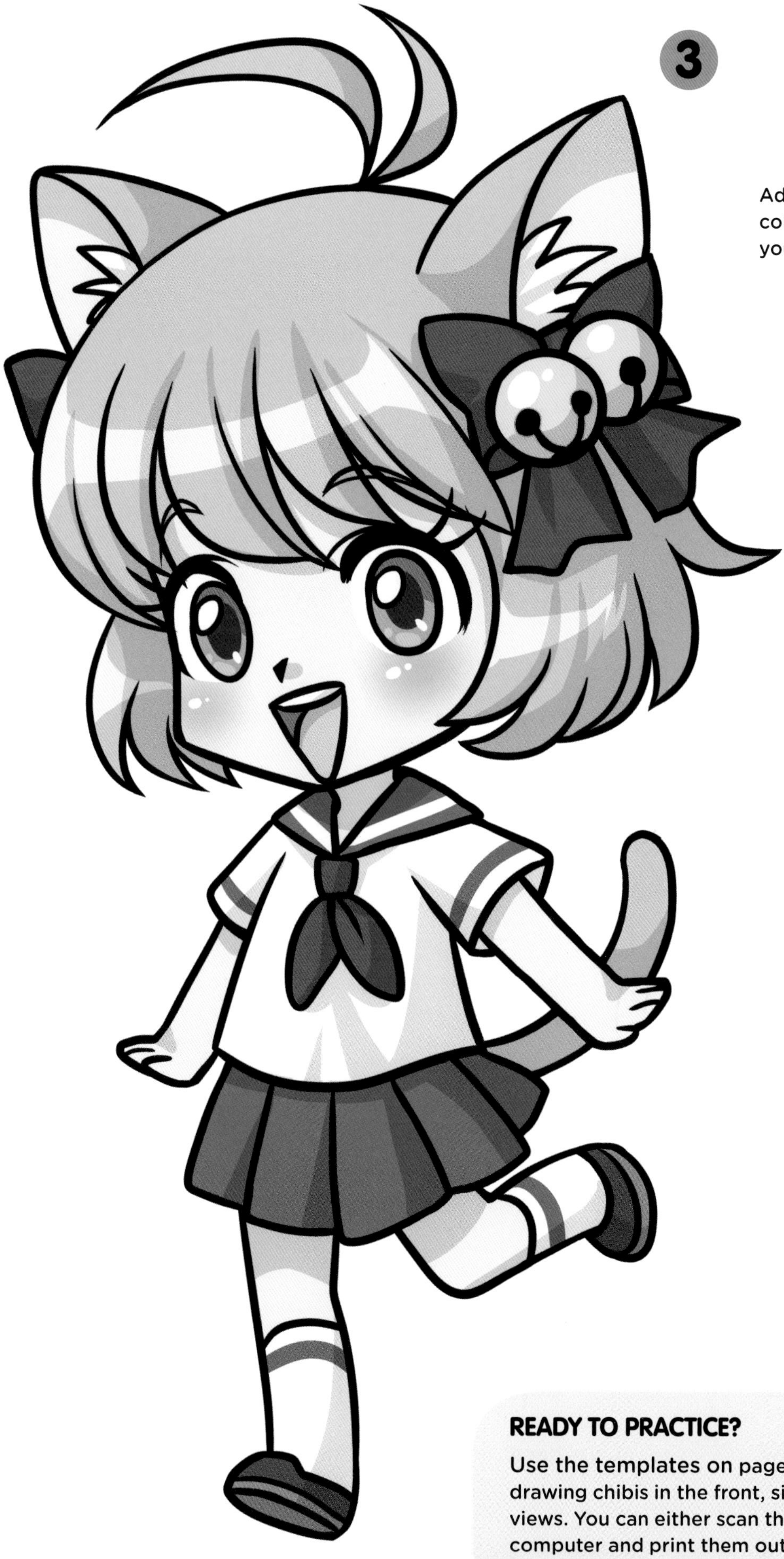

Add Sakura's color, or make up your own!

READY TO PRACTICE?

Use the templates on pages 72–95 to practice drawing chibis in the front, side, and three-quarter views. You can either scan the templates to your computer and print them out or photocopy them from the book.

chibi hands

Drawing hands is one of the most challenging aspects of drawing a person. Hands help express a character's mood, but they're also complex body parts, with joints and fingers that bend and curl in many directions. It's crucial to understand their basic anatomy before drawing them. In this section, you'll learn how to "chibify" regular-sized hands—fortunately, they are much easier to draw! For example, a normal finger has three joints, whereas a chibi finger has only one or none at all. The average chibi hand is a short, chubby version of a normal hand. Some styles, such as the mitten-like hand, don't have fingers; others have fingers that are little nubs. To create a unique look, try combining two or more styles. Experiment with different methods until you find the style you like best.

 **normal fist**

 **chibi fist**

mitten fist

 **mini fist**

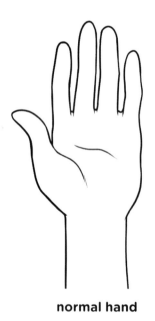 **normal hand**

 **chibi hand**

 **mitten hand**

mini hand

The peace sign is a universally known expression that's also common in anime culture. Let's see how the peace sign looks "chibified"!

NORMAL HAND
The peace sign pose is similar to the fist, except that the index and middle fingers stick straight up to form a V.

CHIBI HAND
The chibi hand has simplified lines and shorter fingers. The last two curled fingers look fused together, and there is no thumbnail.

MITTEN HAND
The mitten hand is even more simplified. The ring and pinky fingers are part of the palm, leaving only the index and middle fingers. The thumb is a curved line, and the wrist is barely noticeable.

MINI HAND
Only a ball-shaped fist and two tiny fingers remain. The wrist disappears with only a slight bulge for the fist.

Now let's review a leaning hand—another common chibi character pose.

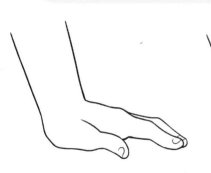 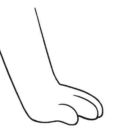  

NORMAL HAND
This side view shows a leaning hand resting on a flat surface. The arm bends upward from the wrist. In a side view, we can only see one side of the hand, the thumb, and two fingers.

CHIBI HAND
In the chibi version, knuckles and joints aren't visible. Remember not to draw chibi fingers all the same length. Here, the middle finger is slightly longer than the index finger. The thumb and pinky shouldn't be longer than the middle finger.

MITTEN HAND
Here the fingers are meshed together into one shape, and the thumb is even more simplified.

MINI HAND
Here the hand is triangular with a couple of lines to indicate the fingers. The bottom of the hand is almost completely straight.

chibi feet

Some artists find that drawing feet is more challenging than drawing hands. For other artists, the opposite is true. Don't get discouraged if one is more challenging for you than the other. Drawing hands and feet requires practice to make them look natural. Like hands, chibi feet begin as simplified versions of normal feet. The foot shortens, toes shrink and get stubbier, and joints—even the ankle—disappear.

Below is a typical standing three-quarter pose that is common in manga and anime.

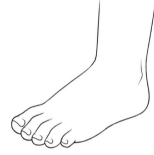 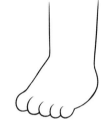 

NORMAL FOOT
The normal foot is typically long, with toes that curl slightly at the joints. The toenails and ankle bone are visible, and the heel has slight definition.

CHIBI FOOT
The chibi foot is a simplified version of the normal foot. The length is shorter, the toes are more rounded, and the joints aren't visible at all.

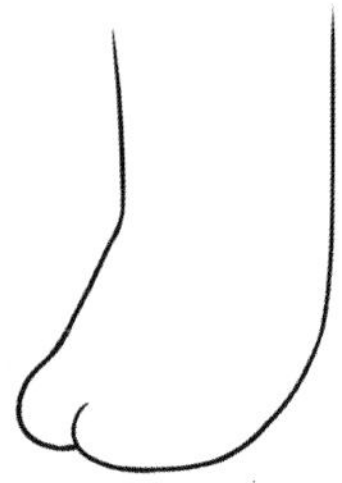

MITTEN FOOT
The mitten foot shows the smaller toes melded into one shape with only a line indicating the big toe. The ankle is also the same width as the leg and foot. Some chibi feet look like this when wearing socks.

MINI FOOT
The mini foot is more simplified and abstract. Its length is shorter, and the toes are little nubs. The ankle and leg are one form.

Now let's observe the bottom of the foot. You may see this pose when a character is about to take a step or descend stairs.

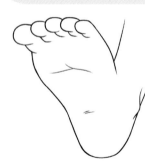 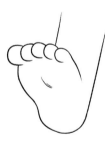  

NORMAL FOOT
Although the bottom of the feet are essentially flat, sometimes drawing them is challenging. The toes curl in at the center of each toe. Additional lines show the foot's contours.

CHIBI FOOT
The bottom of the chibi foot is simplified. Toes are round and ball-shaped, and the joints are not visible. A few simple lines suggest the ball of the foot.

MITTEN FOOT
The mitten foot doesn't change much from the bottom angle.

MINI FOOT
Triangular nubs denote the toes, including the big toe, which is the same size as the others. This is a stylistic choice, so feel free to experiment.

chibi Legs

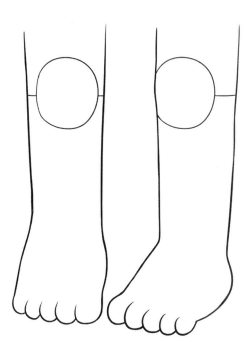

CHIBI LEGS
Average chibi feet have standard legs: short, thick with little to no muscle definition. Indents at the top of the foot and a slight curve outward at the heel help distinguish the feet from the legs.

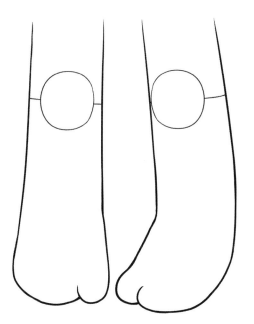

MITTEN LEGS
With mitten-style feet, legs are usually wider at the ankle and become gradually more narrow moving up the thighs. These legs have no muscle definition. The ankles are barely indicated with a slight bend at the top of the foot. Dolls and stuffed animals also have this same leg style.

EXERCISE YOUR CREATIVITY!
Art is about experimentation, so feel free to mix and match leg and feet styles. You might even come up with a style that is uniquely yours!

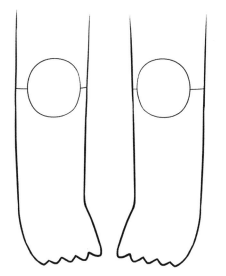

MINI LEGS
Like mitten legs, mini legs have no muscle definition because they are simplified. The width is consistent the entire length of the leg, which is straight and cylinder-like. The ankles are absorbed into the width of the legs and feet, and knees aren't rendered at all; however, keep in mind where they are if you need to bend the legs.

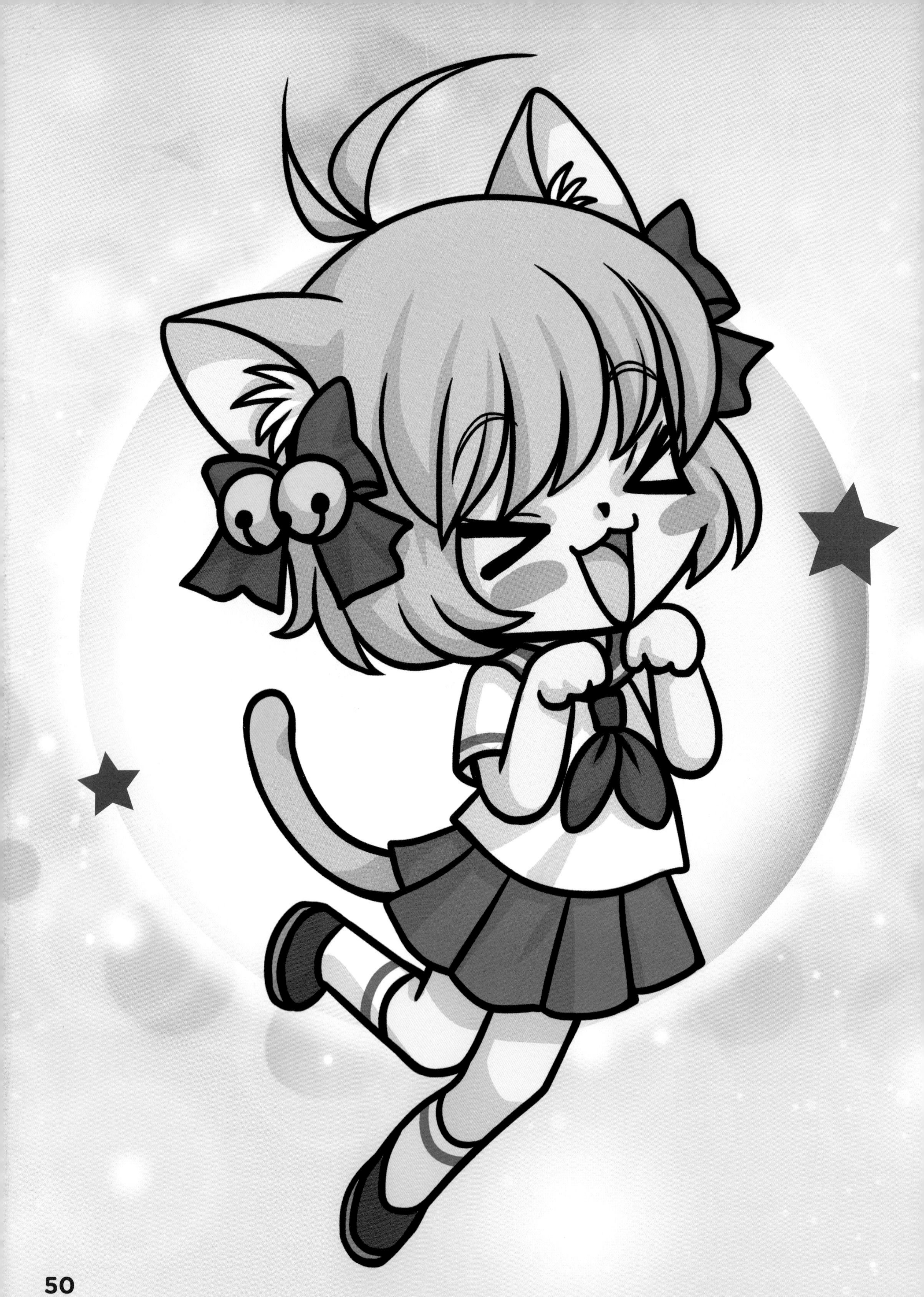

CHAPTER 2
chibis in action

basic poses

Because of their simplicity, chibis rely as heavily on poses to express emotions as they do on facial expressions. Knowing how to draw a variety of poses gives you far more options when conveying your characters' moods. As you know, chibis generally have fewer joints and shorter limbs, so their range of poses is a bit limited. But what you can draw (a chibi floating nebulously in space, for example) can be immensely enjoyable. There aren't any strict rules. (Who likes rules, anyway?!) Let's draw our good friend Takashi in a basic standing pose.

Start sketching the basic shapes and guidelines. Draw the arms and feet in a firm stance, but keep the body relaxed.

Next, draw the facial expression, which is slightly cranky in keeping with Takashi's personality. Draw the remaining details, using the guidelines to identify where to draw the clothes and hair.

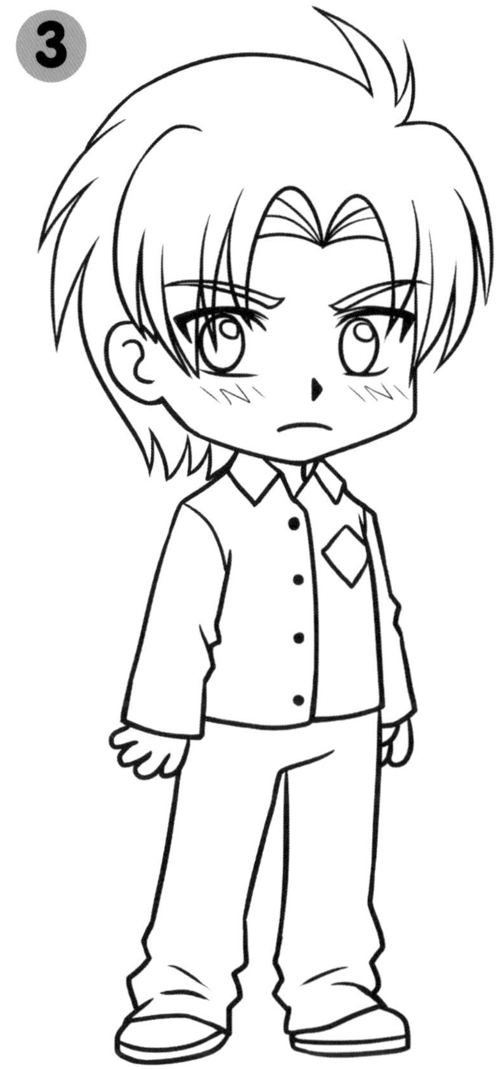

Erase unnecessary sketch lines, and clean up your line art for color.

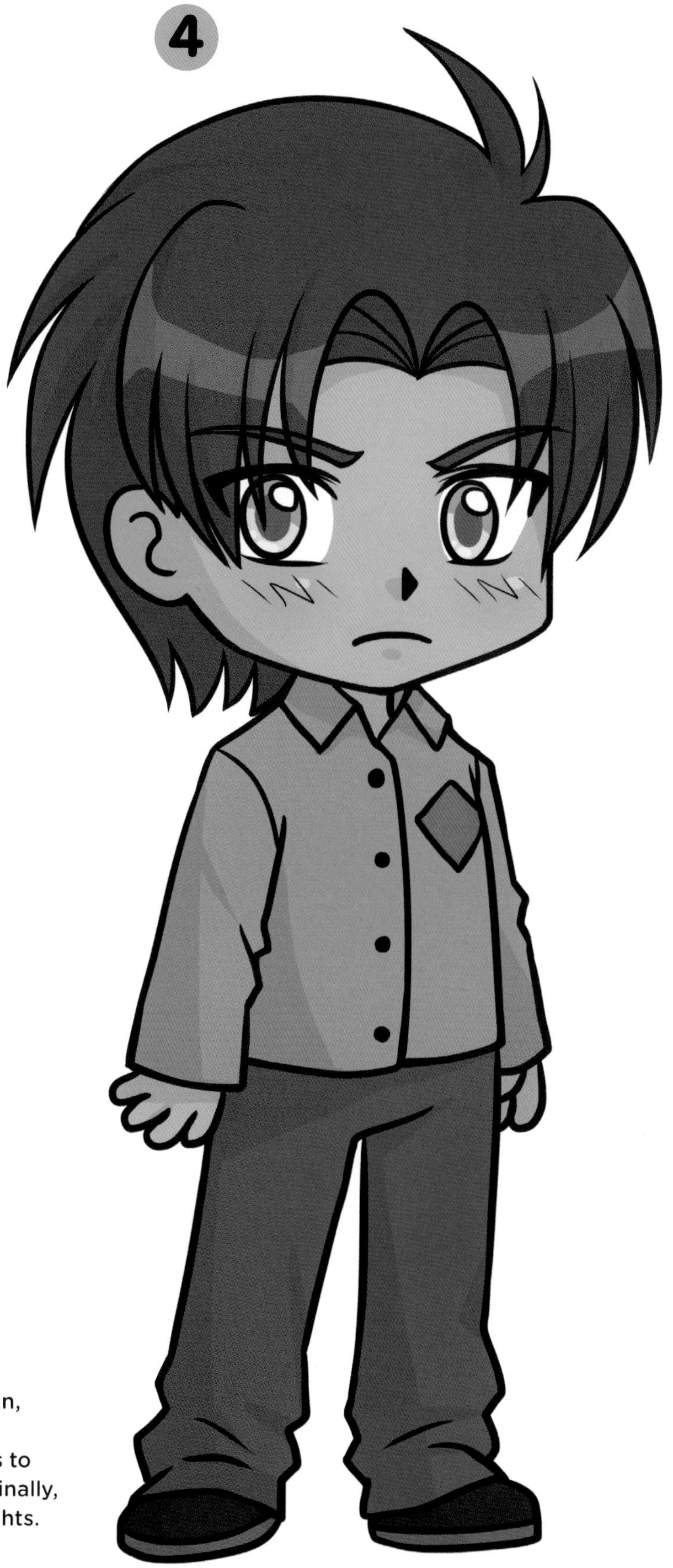

Now add shading to the hair, skin, and clothes. Darken the pupils, adding some brighter highlights to his irises to intensify his stare. Finally, give his hair a few subtle highlights.

THINKING

In this relaxed pose, this chibi sits on his or her knees, with the heels and calves tucked beneath the thighs. The palms rest comfortably on the legs. Perhaps this is a monk or a samurai quietly contemplating life. To draw this pose, start with very basic shapes.

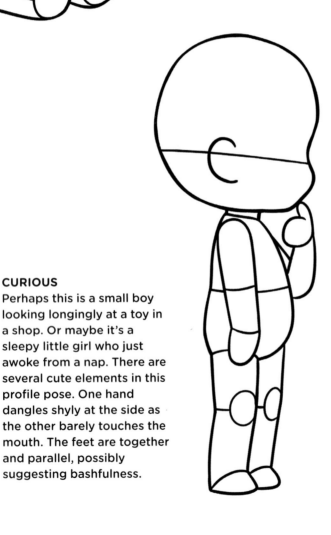

CURIOUS

Perhaps this is a small boy looking longingly at a toy in a shop. Or maybe it's a sleepy little girl who just awoke from a nap. There are several cute elements in this profile pose. One hand dangles shyly at the side as the other barely touches the mouth. The feet are together and parallel, possibly suggesting bashfulness.

SITTING

In this pose, the chibi sits demurely, with both hands tucked in the lap. The knees touch, the toes face each other, and the back is straight. The head is straight, with the chin angled slightly downward. Notice how each body part contributes to the overall pose.

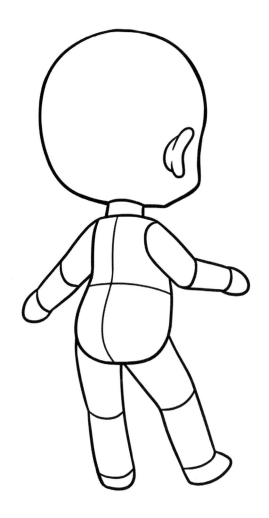

FLOATING BACK

This is the *nearly* back view of a floating pose. The back of head is mostly visible, and the ear looks three-dimensional. The left arm and left leg appear farther away than the right arm and right leg. The arms seem casually raised to suggest floating. The feet also splay slightly outward, ready to land on the ground. This is a good pose for a flying character, who is landing after an excursion in the night sky.

FLOATING FRONT

This pose depicts a chibi seemingly drifting in an empty space. Use it for a chibi astronaut floating in space, a deep-sea diver exploring the ocean, or as the ending point of a leaping pose. Notice how the head and torso angle toward the left, with the bottom half of the body leaning forward and the top half leaning backward. Both arms reach out to maintain balance, and both legs splay outward in preparation for the feet to land.

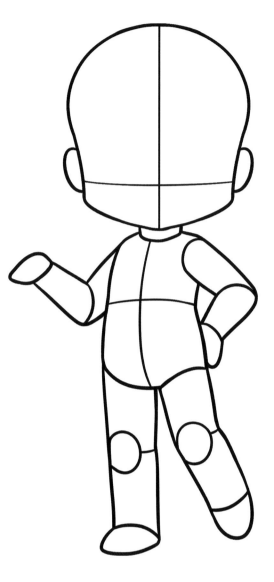

EXCITED
This chibi is just giddy with excitement! The torso is straight, and the vertical guidelines line up. The mood is communicated by the position of the arms, which are bunched together in front of the chest, and the hands touching at the mouth. One leg stands firmly on the ground as the other kicks up from the knee. What does the body language say about the kind of facial expression this chibi should have?

SPEAKING
This pose could be used for a teacher or a spokesperson. Because the pose is intended to exude confidence, both the head and torso should be straight. The face looks directly at the viewer, so consider the facial expression carefully. Notice how one arm is propped on the side of the hip and the other extends outward. Finally, one leg bears most of the weight and the other shifts slightly.

VICTORY

The model is clearly elated for coming out on top and making a V for victory. Perhaps this character is a runner who just won the race and is posing for photos. The strong torso and head and straight legs give this stance an air of confidence. And one arm propped on the hip suggests that this chibi is proud of a job well done.

DETERMINED

A chibi in this pose could be ready to rumble or about to save someone from a burning building. Once again, the head and torso are erect to demonstrate confidence and bravery. The arms and legs are bent, ready to pounce into action. And one foot sits slightly behind the other to create a solid and steady pose and to add perspective to the stance.

action poses

Action poses are snapshots of a character mid movement. (Think of a photo taken two seconds after someone springs off a diving board.) Let's draw Sakura in a supercute jumping pose that lets us know she is over-the-moon happy.

1

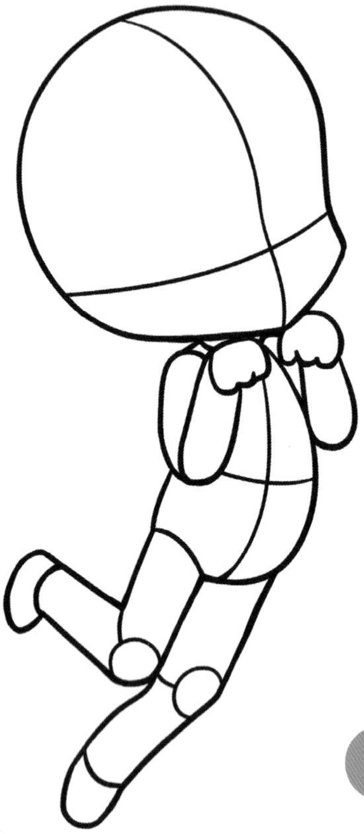

Begin with the basic shapes and guidelines. To achieve Sakura's cat girl pose, tuck both hands under her chin and curl her hands inward so they resemble paws. Make sure her feet are off the ground so she appears to be mid jump. Raise one leg high behind her for added charm.

2

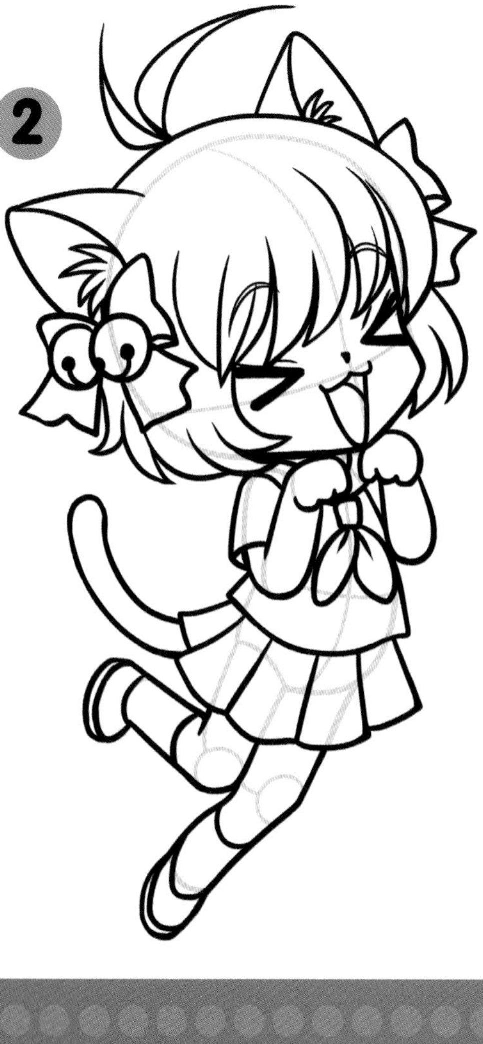

After the basic shapes and guidelines are set, draw in the hair, facial features, clothes, and shoes.

3

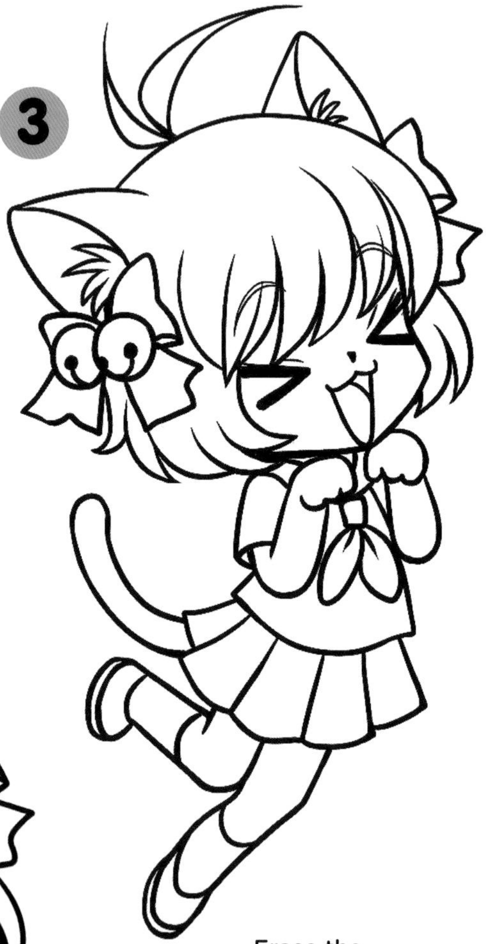

Erase the guidelines, and clean up your line art for color.

4

Now add color and shading, keeping the light source in mind. The shading here is mostly on Sakura's left, which means the light source is on her front-right side. Finally, add highlights to her hair so it appears glossy.

Take a minute to study the red line of action in each of the following poses. The line of action is an imaginary line extending from the head to the spine (or the feet). Its purpose is to provide a general idea of the direction and flow of a character's pose. Drawing the line of action first is a handy way to figure out how and where to place the arms and legs.

JUMPING
Pay attention to the way the legs, arms, and head line up with the shape of the torso to create one fluid movement throughout the body. The back is arched so the belly sticks out and the hips jut slightly forward. The head tilts up and slightly back. (You can even imagine a wide-mouthed smile on the face!) Both arms are straight and raised with open palms. Finally, each leg bends at the knees so this character appears to be jumping off the ground.

RUNNING
In this pose, the upper body angles slightly forward in the same direction the character moves, and the head tilts upward. Mimicking real-life running, the arms are in opposite positions to maintain balance. The hands are balled into fists. The left leg extends forward, with the foot nearly striking the ground. The right leg is lifted high behind the character's body.

GIGGLING

Characters in this pose can be drawn sitting on a flat surface or floating. (Imagine this character as a fairy fluttering in the sky, giggling at something she finds amusing!) In this pose, the torso is bent in at the waist. One arm is straight and extends downward. The other arm bends, with a hand touching her mouth, as though she's concealing a smile. One leg bends with the knee raised higher than the other leg to create contrast and make the image more dynamic.

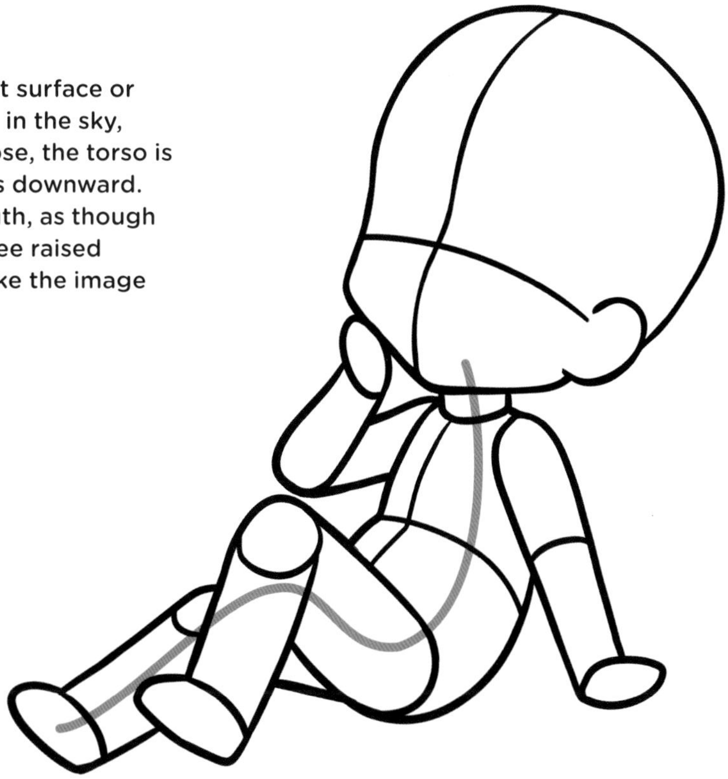

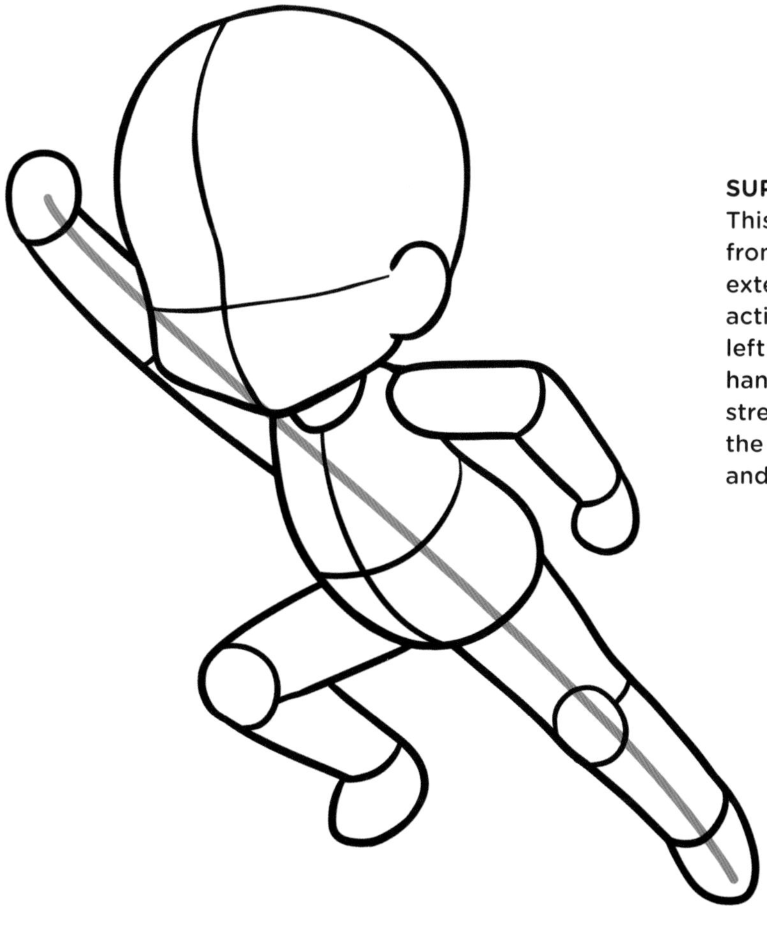

SUPERHERO

This strong line of action extends all the way from the fist in the raised arm to the toes of the extended leg. All the body parts support the action pose by lining up with each other. The left arm bends and thrusts backward, with the hand in a fist to demonstrate the character's strength. The right arm extends straight above the character's head. The left leg is straight, and the right leg bends at the knee.

CHEERLEADER

Draw this pose in a front view. Because the character is jumping, the body and head are straight and aligned with each other. Both arms extend straight outward in a "Y" shape from the torso. The hands bend at the wrists; the palms are open and face upward. Both legs extend outward—the arms and legs together should make an "X" shape, and the knees bend slightly for a more natural look.

FLYING

The body parts are aligned in a straight line of action. The upper torso angles upward, following the line of the head. Notice the similarities between these arms and the arms in the running pose. The fully extended leg continues the line of action, making the body appear long and streamlined. The other leg bends at the knee and tucks into the stomach and chest to suggest intense speed.

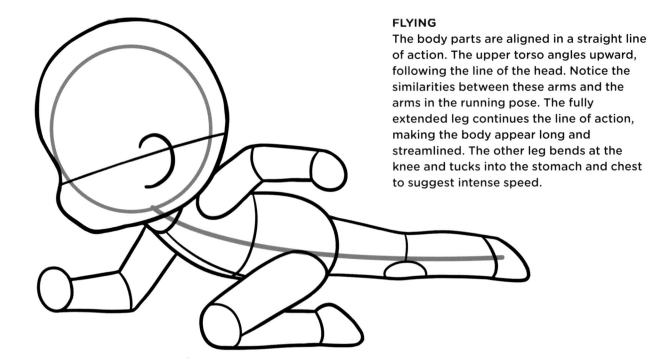

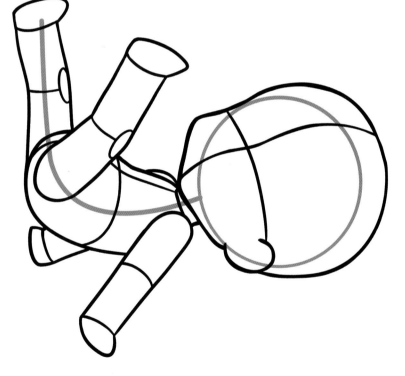

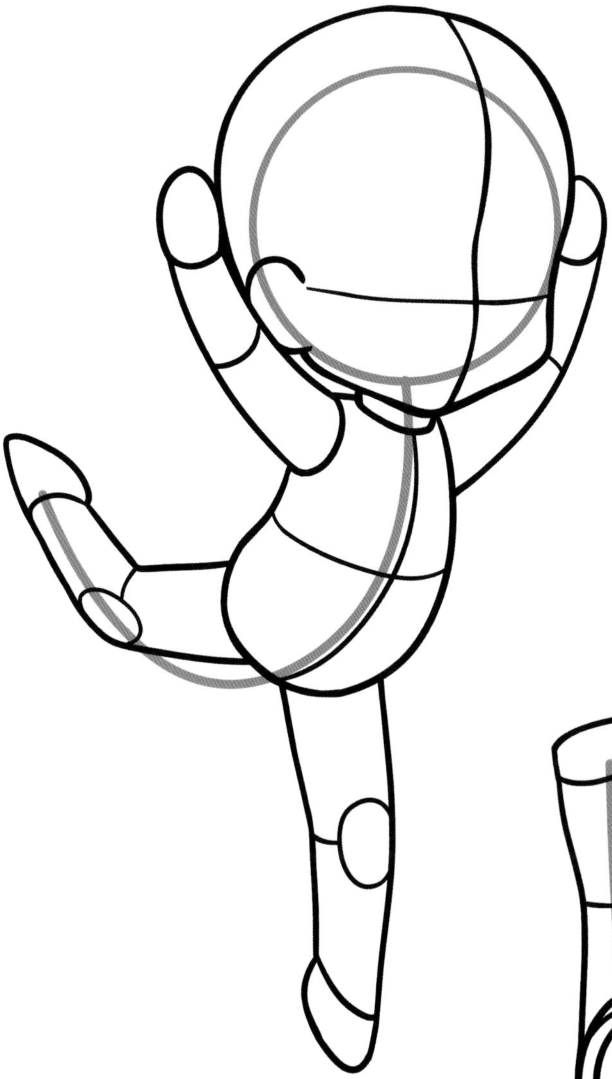

DANCING
The line of action indicates the flow of the body. The torso is straight and aligned with the head. The hips tilt toward the rear to support the legs. Both arms curve slightly as they lift upward in a ballet-like pose. The hands are open and extended, with palms facing inward. The chibi's left leg extends straight through the toe, which is pointed at the tip. The right leg bends at the knee and raises high behind the character—a display of a dancer's flexibility. Make sure the toes point gracefully to complete the line of the pose.

EXERCISE YOUR CREATIVITY!
Make a list of actions you do often: swim, walk the dog, jumping jacks, karate, etc. Then make the poses while someone photographs you, or you can draw yourself as you make these poses in the mirror. Designate the line of action for each, and break down the poses into basic shapes.

TUMBLING
The torso aligns with the head, but at an extreme angle to depict the sense of falling. The arms extend behind the character, as if he or she is trying to break the fall. Both legs have lost their footing, so they're flailing in front of the character. Positioning one leg closer to the body than the other makes the pose more dynamic.

super-chibis

Super-chibis (also called mini-chibis) look even smaller and more simplified than average ones. Check out the basic shapes that make up the front view of the super-chibi below. The head is huge and is almost half the super-chibi's total height! The body takes up the other half, and body parts are even smaller and shorter. Super-chibis have a doll-like appearance.

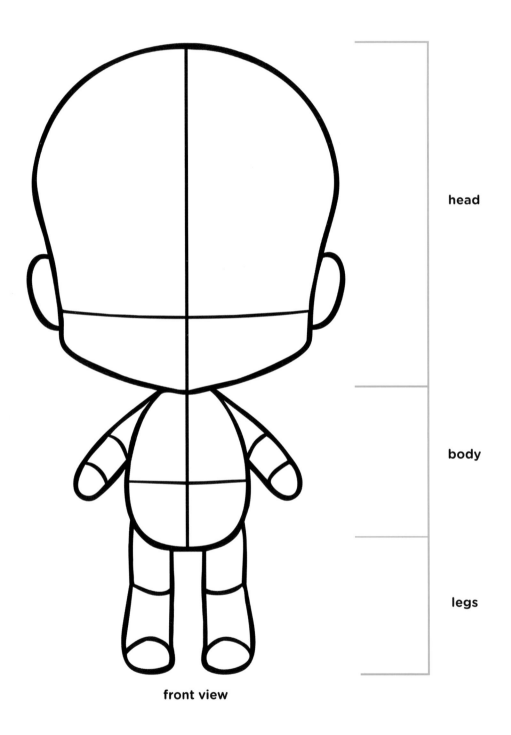

head

body

legs

front view

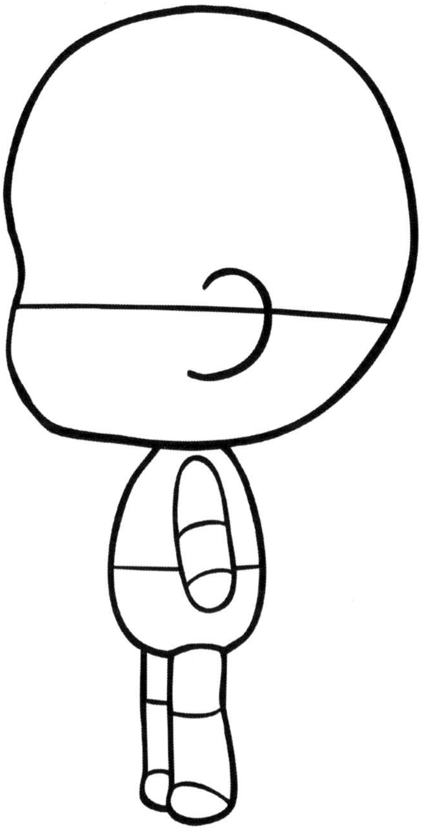

side view

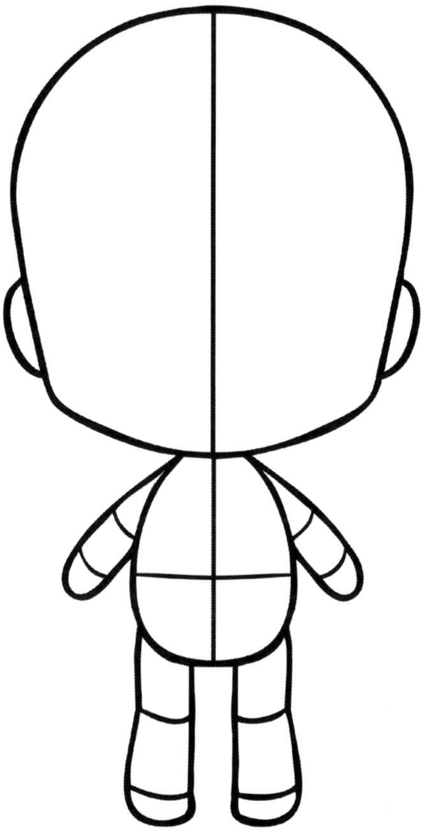

back view

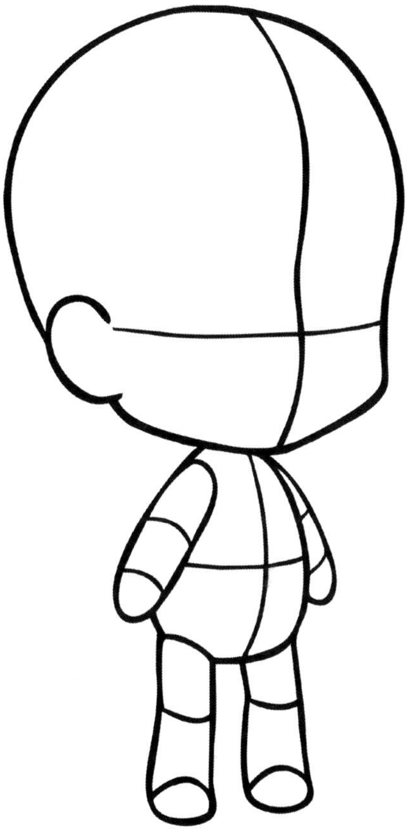

¾ view

Above is the super-chibi from other angles. The guidelines on the face and body show which direction each form faces. Super-chibis don't typically have necks, which makes them look cuter and more compact. Legs are usually stout at the thighs, narrowing to little rounded tips. Some super-chibis don't even have elbows or knees. Some have nub-like, mitten-shaped hands, rather than fingers. Super-chibis are worlds of fun to draw—especially when you experiment!

tip

When adding outfits or accessories to a super-chibi, keep patterns and textures simple. Super-chibis are so small already that adding excess detail becomes distracting.

super-chibi

Because super-chibi body parts are simplified, the hands and feet nearly meld with the arms and legs. Super-chibis typically don't have ankles and wrists either. This super-chibi doesn't have a neck, as her body is too short to accommodate one. Her mouth is large, and her huge eyes take up most of the face. Some super-chibis have noses; others do not.

1

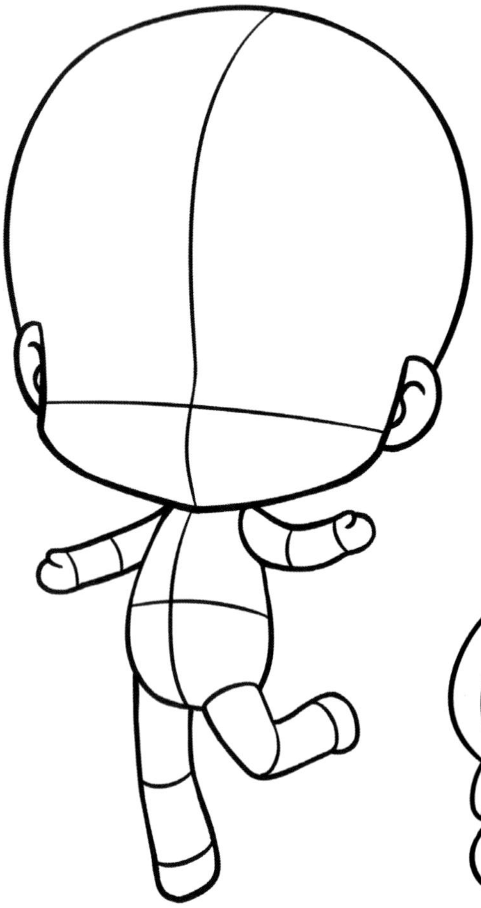

Start with basic shapes and guidelines. Notice how big the head is! Her arms and legs are super short. Her hands are little nubs with tiny thumbs. Her feet are smaller and only a tad wider than her legs.

2

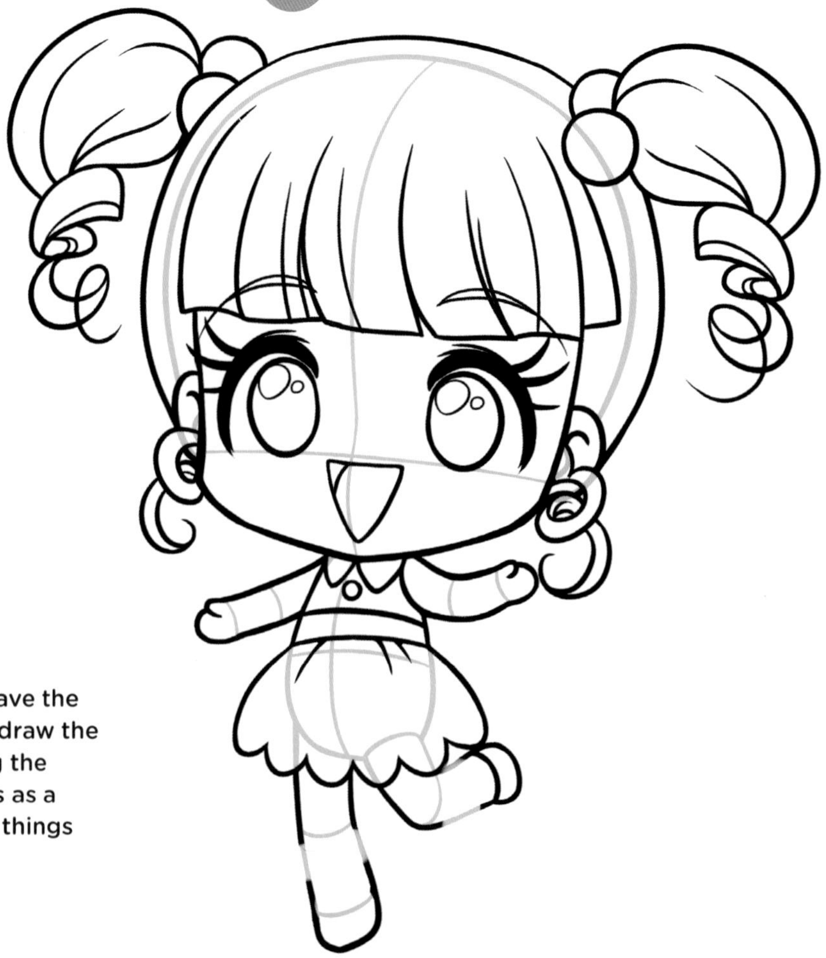

When you have the pose down, draw the details using the basic shapes as a guide. Keep things simple!

3

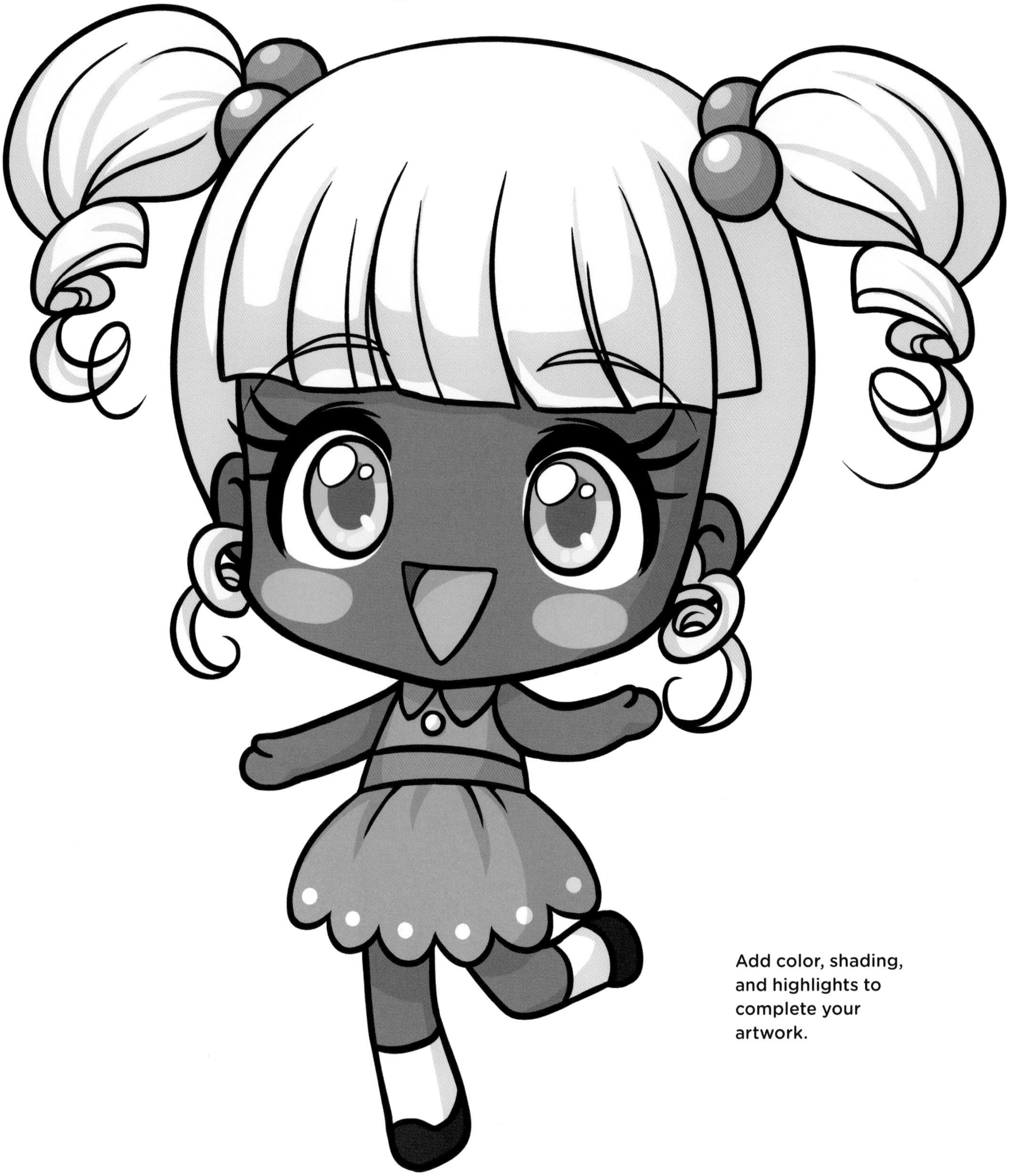

Add color, shading, and highlights to complete your artwork.

super-chibis in action

Super-chibi body types may be shorter and have limited motion, but they still can demonstrate tons of personality and action through their poses. This super-chibi appears to be running after a ball. His forward-leaning posture and exaggerated pose make the illustration all the more convincing.

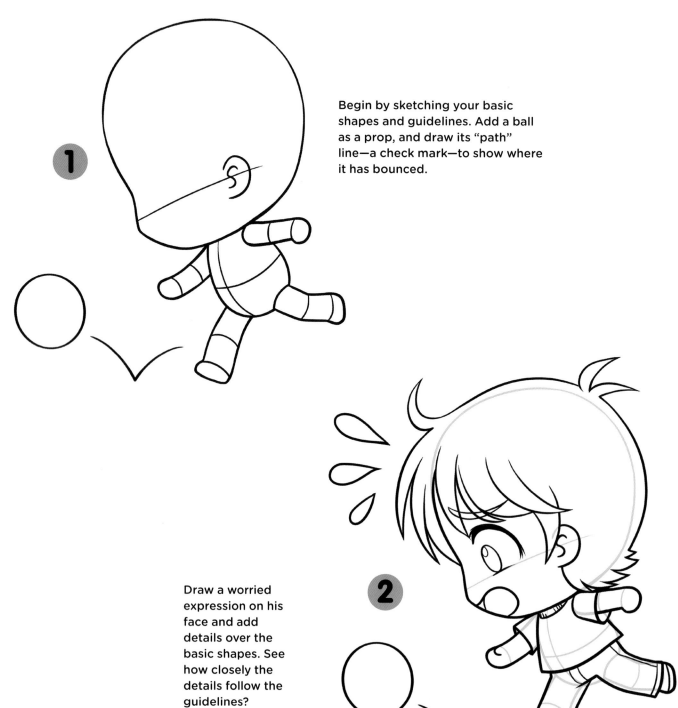

Begin by sketching your basic shapes and guidelines. Add a ball as a prop, and draw its "path" line—a check mark—to show where it has bounced.

Draw a worried expression on his face and add details over the basic shapes. See how closely the details follow the guidelines?

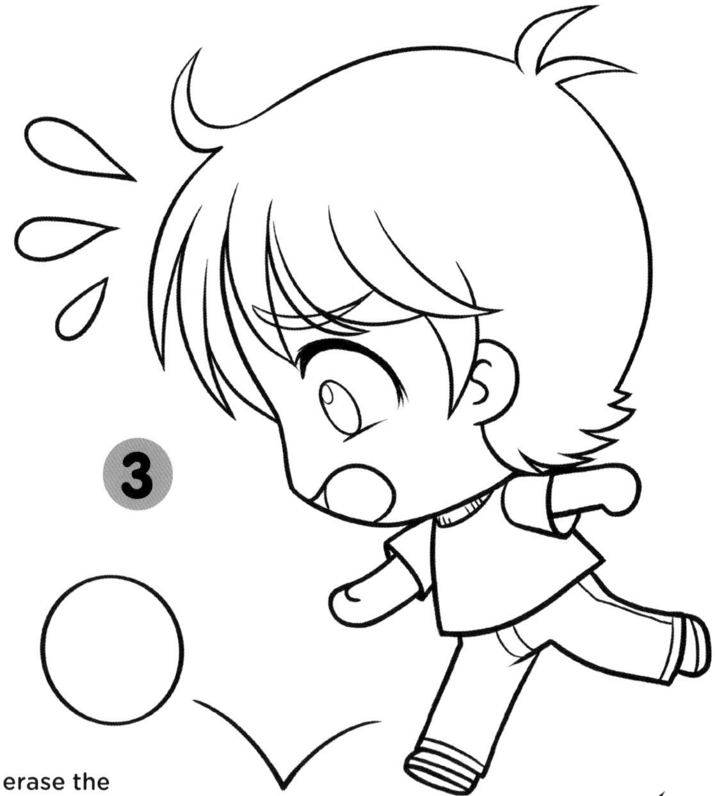

Now erase the guidelines before moving to color.

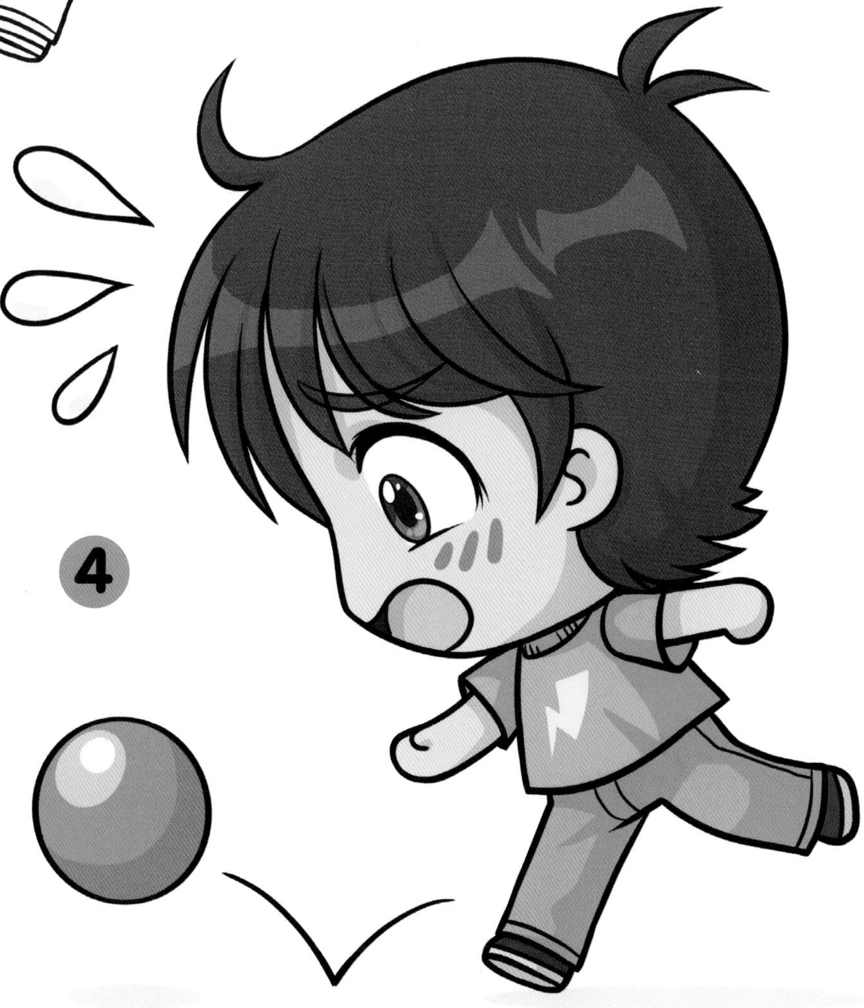

tip

Add light-colored circles below the character to serve as shadows. This gives the drawing depth.

Add the basic colors. Then add shading to the hair, skin, clothes, and ball. Highlights add depth and dimension to the ball. Finally, add highlights around the eyeball and darken the pupil.

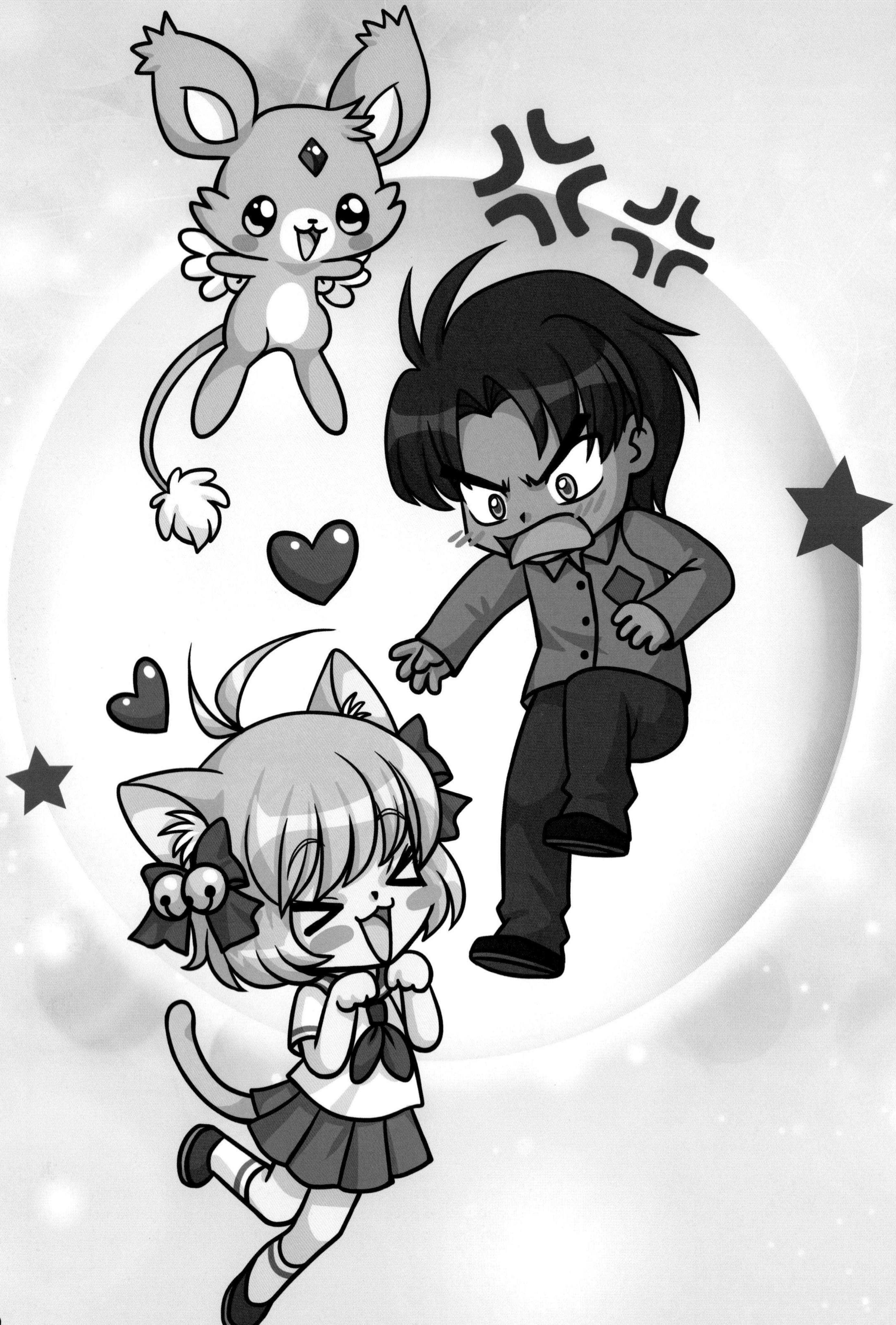

CHAPTER 3
chibi TEMPLATES

head

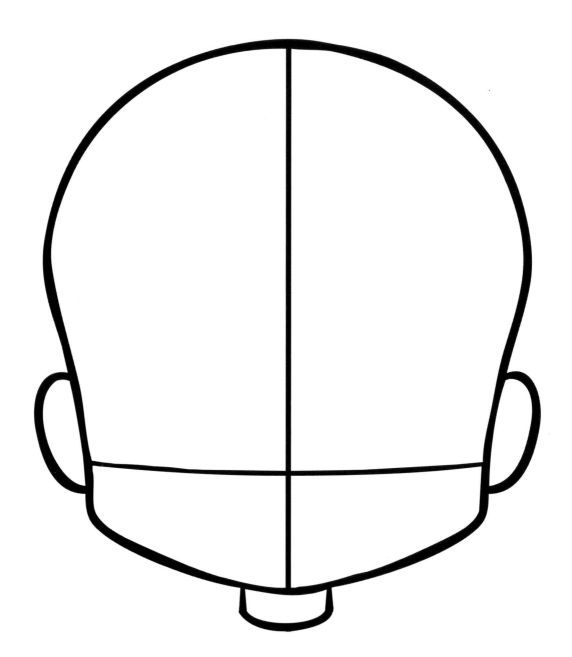

head side view

front view

side view

³/₄ view

back view

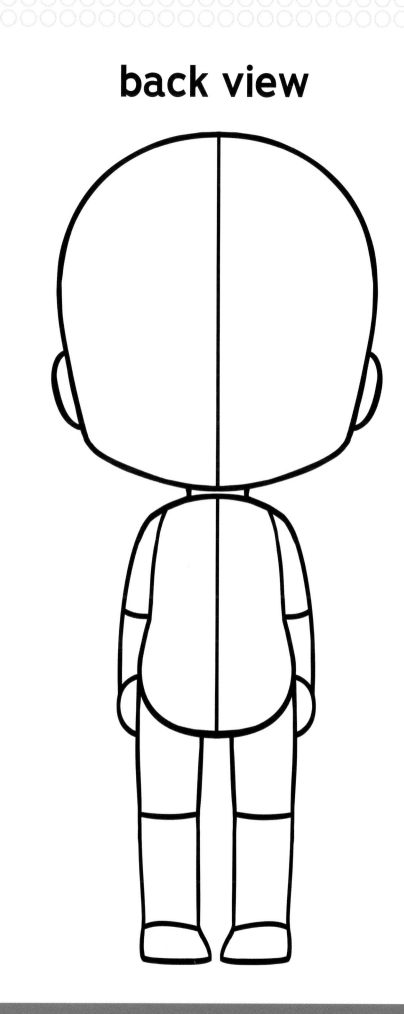

running

jumping

thinking

curious

Laying back

fLoating back

excited

speaking

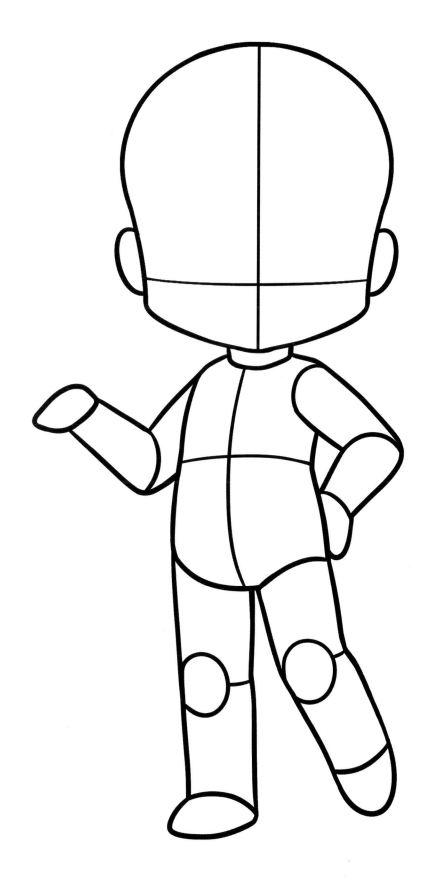

sitting

victorious

determined

hopping

giggLing

super-chibi front view

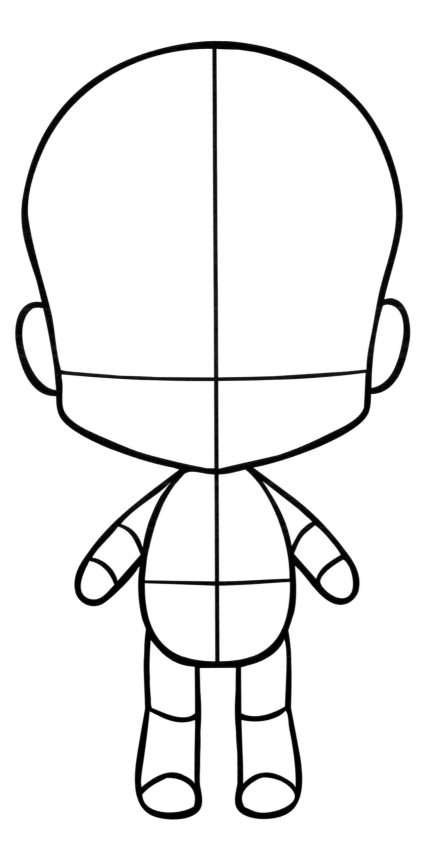

super-chibi side view

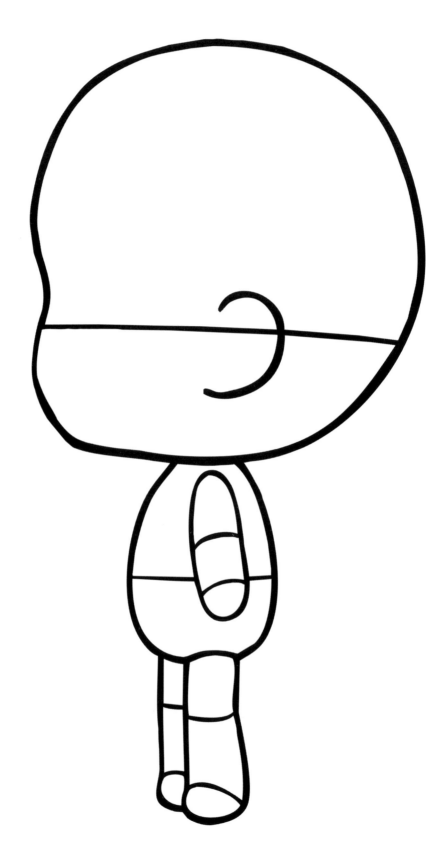

super-chibi ¾ view

super-chibi back view

super-chibi in action

about the artists

Samantha Whitten is an independent artist who specializes in adorable illustrations. She has spent all of her life drawing and has pursued a career in illustration and graphic design, learning on her own and dabbling in a variety of projects. She earns a living by selling a unique range of self-produced products featuring her artwork, employing a cute and fun style that appeals to all ages, as well as illustrating a web comic in her spare time. Visit her website at www.littlecelesse.com for more!

Jeannie Lee's art education includes more than seven years of instruction under contemporary Western artist Ji Young Oh, as well as two years studying traditional character animation at California Institute of the Arts. Jeannie has worked for Gaia Interactive, Marvel Entertainment, Inc., TOKYOPOP, and UDON Entertainment.